ESSAY ON SLAVERY;

AS CONNECTED WITH THE MORAL AND PROVIDENTIAL GOVERNMENT OF GOD;

AND AS AN ELEMENT OF

CHURCH ORGANIZATION.

WITH

MISCELLANEOUS REFLECTIONS ON THE SUBJECT OF SLAVERY.

BY THOMAS J. TAYLOR.

For what the law could not do, in that it was weak through the flesh, God sending his own Son in the likeness of sinful flesh, and for sin, condemned sin in the flesh: that the righteousness of the law might be fulfilled in us, who walk not after the flesh, but after the Spirit.--ROMANS viii, 3, 4.

New-York:
PUBLISHED FOR THE AUTHOR,
200 Mulberry-street.

INTRODUCTION.

In this age of improvement, and in a world abounding with great, greater, and greatest men, we feel no small degree of embarrassment at the thought of passing the ordeal of public scrutiny in the character of an author. Such an idea, in the commencement of those sections which form the first part of this work, was not entertained, no, not even dreamed of, either in our sleeping or waking hours. Circumstances, however, have somewhat strangely conspired to lead matters on to this end, and which are as follows:—

Since the days of our youth we have been an unworthy member of the Methodist Episcopal Church. In the recent agitation of the abolition question, (which is one with which we sympathize, when restricted to proper limits,) the leaders of that movement, in its ultra form, together with those who follow in the wake, have seemed to feel and act as if they thought they had a special mission from God to denounce—not only as thieves and robbers, but as the synagogue of Satan, and many other like grave charges — those churches, and the members of those churches which, as an evil, tolerate the relation as in agreement with the Scriptures. Having been thus personally, repeatedly assailed, both from the pulpit and the press, as also the Church with which we stand connected, in the acceptance of challenges loudly and frequently given, we volunteered the defence of our Church against the charge of pro-slaveryism. Our first number was published, and the second forwarded for publication, and as it was retained on hand some four weeks before the editor leaked out his purpose to rule me out, by this time we had written the greater part of what is embraced in the first part of this work.

Having thus made some progress in the investigation, we desired, for our own satisfaction, as we should have opportunity from other cares, to push our inquiries through the subject, and ascertain, so far as our capacity would bear us out in its examination, whether or not we were in error, in the views entertained relative to the strictly Scriptural position of the Church.

It thus being known to some, who desired the further publication of my manuscript; and to others, on whom the author obtruded some of his numbers for critical remarks as to doctrine, &c., and who thought it deserved a more permanent existence than an ephemeral appearance through the newspaper press, led to their preservation and arrangement in regular and consecutive order, till I had passed through what I regarded the Bible view of the subject, and had made an application of its general teachings, principles, and spirit, on the subject of slavery, to the principles and spirit of the Methodist polity. This being done, other questions, naturally arising out of the subject, pressed themselves on my attention, and which have also been written out, under a conviction that they would be of some importance to the world.

In this way it has swelled up into the shape of a little volume, and, as such, is likely to come into public notice. How extensively, and whether for good or for ill, time must determine. Of one thing, however, we (to change our phraseology before we use up all the capital I's the printer may have) are deeply conscious,—that we have sought only the truth, from the first to the last, and through every intervening step in this investigation; in which we have condensed our thoughts in as small a compass as was practicable, in the examination of this subject in its connexion with God's moral and providential government of the world.

Had we looked merely at the surface of things, we possibly should have been conducted to the same, or like conclusions with the ultra abolitionists of the day; namely, that slavery is too outstandingly and palpably wrong for a revelation from God, under any circumstances, to make any tolerant allusion to it. Some way then would have been sought to explain away those passages which seem to recognize, and which appear to have been designed for, the government of the relation; and failing in this, as we think every rational mind must do, the next step would have been, as we fear many of them have done, to reject the Scriptures, on account of such monstrous doctrines—so repugnant to our natural rights, and contrary to the voice of reason—as a revelation from God.

But when we endeavour to penetrate and look beneath the surface, and regard it as a part of an administration that takes hold of this world in its connexion with an eternal state; that has more reference to the general than the individual good,—the good of eternity, than the good of time; or, in other words, the greatest good, or greatest amount of good, upon the whole, of all concerned, for both time and eternity; it appears to us not only to be free from the objections alleged against it, but as commending itself to us as an exhibition of the united wisdom and goodness of the moral Governor of the universe, in making the best of circumstances in this as in all other matters connected with the defection of this revolting province of his dominions; and of the truth of which we think the reader will be fully satisfied, by the time he shall have patiently and carefully passed through this little work.

And we would here admonish him, that we think the various parts are so dependent on, and so calculated to illustrate and strengthen each other, that he cannot well understand the subject in its complex character, without an attentive and careful perusal of the whole. We make this remark for the benefit of those who examine a book as many do a newspaper—pick it up, cast a cursory and careless glance over its columns, and if the eye should catch nothing that suits their fastidious taste, throw it aside as a failure. Thoughtful minds—especially at this juncture, when the whole country, from the centre to the circumference, feels its importance; and our national councils, as well as our Church organizations, are trembling to their foundations under its fearful power—will need no such admonition. And if, as we think it does, it shall be found to present the subject in a Scriptural and rational light, and perchance in a somewhat different, if not in an entirely new light, to what it has ever been presented to the world, it will be read with anxiety; and that too without much solicitude as to whence it is, or the peculiarities of its literary dress. This leads us to make a remark in reference to style.

It being the first-born of our pen for public scrutiny, we think we may, with some confidence, claim the indulgence of the sober-minded. And as for the fastidiousness of that taste that will bow down and worship a jackdaw, because dressed in a peacock's feathers, we do not feel a very ponderous solicitude about gratifying it.

That some portions of the work, in point of style, may pass for all our expectations or pretensions, we have no doubt; but that other portions of it, in which we have had to do with men and things that seemed to call for some severity or humour, may be regarded as coarse and common-place, and thus deficient in correct taste, we are fully aware. After all, in this disordered world there are some coarse and vulgar ideas; and as words are the signs of ideas, in writing about them, plain, unpretending men may very naturally fall into this error.

We have felt some anxiety lest, in some of our points of conflict with those avowing slaveholding under all circumstances to be a bar to Church fellowship, we have sometimes expressed ourselves in a way that may be regarded as too severe, and as favouring the principle and practice of slavery. This, however, we hope the intelligent reader, on looking carefully over the whole ground, will be fully satisfied is not our position; and as to what may be the seeming point, it is to be set down either to the weakness of our common nature, or as an honest trial to throw off the weight of an untiring effort, for opinion's sake, to crush and take from us what little reputation we had, because we had, on this subject, the astounding impudence to think and speak for ourselves.

Had we been base enough to suppress our convictions of truth, and surrender the dominion of our conscience to the ignorance, zeal, and bigotry of the Western leaders of the new organization, possibly we might now enjoy a reputable standing among those mistaken brethren. But, in that case, we should have had so great a sense of personal meanness as to be without a conscious sense of personal rectitude in our own bosoms; a sacrifice, with us, entirely too great at which to purchase the favourable regards of any body of men, let alone, so far as we know them, the master spirits and composing elements of that faction.

A thought or two more to the ultra brethren or extreme men—men occupying extreme ground, both in the North and South. Without suffering your feelings to be too much implicated in what you may deem the strong ground taken against your respective positions, examine these pages in the light of a prayerful desire to learn and know, that you may practise the truth; it can do you no harm, but the contrary; to hold and practise the truth will always, on all questions, do us good. If a first reading is not satisfactory, read it over again. And should you find that we are in error, point it out, so as to satisfy us of that error, and we trust we shall have candour enough to renounce and retract it. If, on the other hand, as we think will be the result, you shall be conducted to the conclusion that our position is Scriptural, reasonable, and therefore true, let not the pride of position or opinion deter you from embracing and avowing that truth. Be honest, be independent; and the means which shall have been thus instrumental in leading you to the knowledge of the truth on this subject, recommend to the notice of others; give your aid in promoting its most extensive circulation, that thereby the largest measure of truth may be circulated throughout our whole country. Do not yourselves, nor yet in others, countenance any open or under-handed measures, to prevent either its examination or circulation,—help to let it have free course, run and be glorified; for it is entirely too late in the day to appeal to authority, civil, social, and religious, for the suppression of truth, particularly where that truth is soberly, dispassionately, and respectfully presented. We send it forth to its destiny. May Heaven make its way prosperous and glorious.

THE AUTHOR.

March, 1849.

CONTENTS.

PART FIRST—PRELIMINARY.

SECTION I.

POSITION OF THE CHURCH ON THE SUBJECT OF SLAVERY, AS CONTAINED IN HER ECCLESIASTICAL LAW, STATED . . . . PAGE 11

SECTION II.

OBJECTIONS CONSIDERED:—THAT THE CHURCH IS TOO OBSEQUIOUS TO THE STATE—THE SPIRITUAL TO THE CIVIL POWER 18

SECTION III.

OBJECTIONS CONSIDERED.—THAT THE SAME PRINCIPLES THAT RECEIVE SLAVEHOLDERS INTO THE CHURCH, REQUIRE THE RECEPTION OF HIGHWAYMEN, ADULTERERS, AND MURDERERS 29

SECTION IV.

OBJECTION CONSIDERED.—THAT THE SAME PRINCIPLE THAT RECEIVES SLAVEHOLDERS INTO THE CHURCH, REQUIRES THE RECEPTION OF THE POLYGAMIST 37

SECTION V.

THE RELATION OF SLAVERY, AS TAUGHT IN THE OLD TESTAMENT . . 43

SECTION VI.

THE RELATION OF SLAVERY, AS TAUGHT IN THE NEW TESTAMENT . . 51

SECTION VII.

CRITICAL AUTHORITIES 61

PART SECOND.

ARGUMENTS AGAINST THE DIVINE RIGHT OF SLAVERY, AS AN INSTITUTION OF GOD, OR OF SPECIAL DIVINE APPOINTMENT.

SECTION I.

FIRST ARGUMENT, DRAWN FROM THE LAW OF NATURE 85

SECTION II.

SECOND ARGUMENT, DRAWN FROM THE LAW OF REVELATION—THE RELATION A TEMPORARY REGULATION 94

PART THIRD.

THAT THE SIMPLE RELATION IS NO BAR TO CHURCH FELLOWSHIP.

SECTION I.

FROM THE PRINCIPLES OF GOD'S MORAL AND PROVIDENTIAL GOVERNMENT . . . . PAGE 110

SECTION II.

ITS COMPATIBILITY WITH THE RECTITUDE OF THE DIVINE CHARACTER AND GOVERNMENT 135

SECTION III.

AS SEEN IN ITS PARTICULAR AND RECIPROCAL DUTIES 146

SECTION IV.

AS SEEN IN ITS GENERAL CONDITION 155

SECTION V.

THE PERFECT AGREEMENT OF THE ECCLESIASTICAL POLITY OF THE METHODIST EPISCOPAL CHURCH WITH THE TEACHING OF THE SCRIPTURES, ON THE SUBJECT OF SLAVERY 163

PART FOURTH.

MISCELLANEOUS REFLECTIONS ON DIFFERENT SUBJECTS CONNECTED WITH SLAVERY.

SECTION I.

THOUGHTS ON TRUE WESLEYANISM 172

SECTION II.

ON THE DIVISION OF THE CHURCH 177

SECTION III.

ON THE CONDITION OF AFRICA—AFRICAN SLAVERY AN ACT OF PROVIDENTIAL GOVERNMENT 197

SECTION IV.

ON THE DUTY OF THE GOVERNMENT 205

SECTION V.

A CALM ADDRESS TO THE SOUTH 220

CONCLUSION 267

AN ESSAY ON SLAVERY.

PART I.—PRELIMINARY STATEMENTS.

SECTION I.

POSITION OF THE CHURCH ON THE SUBJECT OF SLAVERY, AS CONTAINED IN HER ECCLESIASTICAL LAW, STATED.

THE Scriptures not only require us to be "ready always to give to every man that asketh us a reason of the hope that is in us, with meekness and fear," which is a rational injunction, and worthy of a religion emanating from God; but they also require or enjoin it upon us, "earnestly to contend for the faith once delivered to the saints." In a world like ours, abounding in free-thinkers, half-thinkers, and no-thinkers, the exhortation cannot but commend itself to our understanding as an important one, and is clearly in evidence that its author regarded the "faith," or religion, taught in the Holy Scriptures, as capable of a triumphant vindication against the objections of all cavillers, of whatever school. The history of the world, thus far, is in proof, that in this confidence he was not mistaken. For notwithstanding the various assaults which in various forms have been made upon it, it still exists; and instead of suffering harm by passing the ordeal of rigid, scrutinizing investigation, has gathered strength in every struggle, and brightened in every conflict; so that each succeeding contest in the march of mind serves only to confirm its claims to a heavenly origin, and show its complete adaptation to the weakness, wants, and wisdom of man, in all the variety of his condition. The progress of society, in every stage of mental and moral improvement, proportionately develops its superlative excellency; and warrants the conclusion, that its principles will not only be found suited to the highest possible culture of mind and morals, but also the most, if not the only effectual system, by which the character of man, in these lofty and distinguishing attributes of his nature, can be fully developed. The fact that its ranks have furnished, and still continue to furnish, the most elevated and finished specimens of human greatness that the history of the world presents, is indubitable evidence of the truth of the above proposition. And with this commanding proof before us of its inherent practical utility, that it should have, ever and anon, to be contending with the embattled hosts of determined opposition, would be a problem of difficult solution, but for the light reflected on this and similar questions by the language of the prophet, when he tells us that "the whole head is sick, and the whole heart faint;" and that men "do not know," because they do not consider;—the want of reflection being the cause of their ignorance; and that ignorance the cause of their opposition. In this, and similar language found in the Bible, is disclosed the true secret of all opposition to the principles and measures of the divine administration. The mind being enfeebled, and the heart corrupted by sin, in our stupid infatuation and heedlessness, though frequently called upon to "hear" and "consider," we will not give ourselves the trouble to think; choosing rather to walk in the sight of our own eyes, and after the desire of our own hearts, than to hear and receive the word of heavenly instruction, which would redeem us from error, and guide us into all truth.

A recent attack, insidiously made upon Christianity, is in the denunciation of the Church and Ministry,—the divinely instituted and appointed instrumentalities by which to convert the world, and build it up in the faith of the Gospel: and the reasons assigned are, first, the connexion of the Church with Slavery, in receiving, and retaining in her communion, persons in that relation; and, secondly, that the Ministry, as the prominent actors and messengers of the churches, instead of rebuking and wholly excluding it from the Church of God, connive at and lend their sanction to this state of things. Other matters enter into, or are embraced in, the general complaint; some of which in an unqualified, and others in a qualified, sense, have our cordial approval; such as intemperance, war, &c. These, we repeat, mainly constitute the reasons for the onset; and form the basis of urgent, inflammatory, derisive, and denunciatory appeals, loud and long, in the public ear, against the Church, and against the Ministry and the Christianity of the present age. Especially in the slavery aspect of the question, does the trump of opposition wax louder and louder; with the cry of "Down with the Church!" and "Down with the Ministry!" as the chief machinations and instruments of his Satanic majesty (if their creed allows his existence) for carrying on, in this sin-disordered world, his work of ruin and death.

And in this particular view of the question, professed Christians, in their individual and organized capacities, join hand in hand with infidelity; at least so far as to proscribe, and hand over to the fatherly care of old Apollyon, all those churches, as well as individuals, who, under any circumstances, tolerate the relation as being compatible with a creditable profession of religion. Hence the recent organization of religious bodies, making it under all circumstances a bar to church fellowship; and the untiring effort of those organizations, for opinion's sake, to bring into contempt and infamy all those, whether individuals or churches, who differ from them in the general scriptural view of this vexed question.

We hear it from the pulpit and the platform, we read it from the press, that society would be vastly benefited if the convicts of our penitentiaries were turned loose upon the world, and the ministry, with a few honourable exceptions, (that is, those who embrace their peculiar views,) were shut up in their stead; and if any mean or wicked thing has been done in a distant neighbourhood, branded with peculiar marks of atrocity, enormity, and depravity, it is at once attributed to some pro-slavery class-leader, deacon, elder, or preacher. And the churches also come in for a full share of the same exaggerated and denunciatory detraction. They are declared to be the "synagogue of Satan,"—the "mother of harlots," &c., &c.; and are represented by the most coarse and vulgar anecdotes; such as give evidence of a determination the most heated, as well as the most untiring, to heap all the odium that language and circumstances can bring upon her, and thereby bring her into such disrepute as to become, instead of "the praise and glory of the earth," "a byword and hissing" to all intelligence,—hoping thereby, as they claim, to effect her reform; but, as we fear, and we think not without evidence, her final overthrow.

The same principle of proscription is carried out in a variety of resolutions, at their various meetings; one of which was the remote cause of this essay, and which in substance, if not verbatim, was as follows:—

"*Resolved*, That the churches that retain slave-holding are the greatest barriers to freedom, or bulwarks of the system; and that, in so doing, they yield the supremacy of the law of God, and substitute measures of human policy and interest."

Now to the principle involved in this resolution, namely, that the reception and retention of persons in the relation into the Church, all things else being right, is a measure of human policy, in contravention of the Divine law, and brands the church so practising as pro-slavery, we enter our solemn protest, and shall proceed to give the reasons that govern our faith in this matter, particularly in reference to the Methodist Episcopal Church, of which we have had the honour to be an unworthy member since the days of our boyhood.

The reader will first indulge us in the statement of a principle, or discrimination, that appears to us to lie deep at the foundation of this momentous question; one that, so far as our reading is concerned, has been entirely overlooked, and is of superlative importance to its correct understanding; namely, that slavery in its incipiency, and slavery as an element of organized society, are different things; or, in other words, the relation of the parties thereto, in its different stages, involves widely different degrees of moral turpitude. The man who kidnaps or steals a man, and the man who buys him when thus stolen, and thus robs him of all his rights, justly deserve the execration of all upright society; human language hardly furnishes adequate terms with which to express the deep enormity attaching to such conduct. And we think it was principally to this stage of the business that Wesley, Clarke, and others referred, when they denounced it in such unmeasured terms. Such a construction is due them, as it harmonizes that which would otherwise appear inconsistent in the views of these great and good men: of which in the sequel. But in a state of organized society, as in the United States,—where the parties who are now connected with slavery had no more to do with the original act of kidnapping, or man-stealing, by which it was first introduced, nor in the enactment of those statutes which authorize, guard, and begird it with all the solemn forms, intricacies, and sanctions of law, than the man in the moon,—their relation thereto, as it appears to us, and must, as we think, so appear to all reasonable men, is widely different. In vain will it here be urged, that the retainer of the stolen goods is equally guilty with the original thief: the circumstances are so widely different, that no sane mind capable of comprehending the question, and appreciating an argument, but will see and feel its fallacy.

Now it is important to keep this discrimination in view, in order to understand properly the Scriptural and anti-slavery bearings of our ecclesiastical law.

The subject of slavery comes up first in what are called our General Rules, where the positive and negative qualifications of persons applying for membership among us are set forth in detail. Among them is the following:—"The buying and (or) selling men, women, and children, with an intention to enslave them,"—which prohibits the person or persons so practising from a place in our communion. This is slavery in its incipiency,—the commencement of this diabolical business,—where we think the greatest guilt attaches. And how a law which lays the axe at the root of this tree of iniquity—which strikes at the very foundation of the whole matter, and cuts off all persons so offending from a place among us—can be regarded as a pro-slavery measure, we cannot understand.

In the second place, the Discipline pronounces upon the general character of slavery, whether in its incipiency, or as an element of organized society, as a "great evil." And by what process of reasoning we can arrive at the conclusion, that a statute thus fixing its veto upon slavery, as a "great evil," is pro-slavery, we cannot perceive.

Next comes that part of the law which treats especially of slavery as an element of organized society; and which bars any slaveholder from official station in the Church, where the laws of the State in which he lives will admit of emancipation, and permit the liberated slave to enjoy freedom; and works the forfeiture of the ministerial character of any travelling preacher who in any way becomes the owner of a slave or slaves, unless he execute, if practicable, a legal emancipation, conformably to the laws of the State in which he may reside; and, further, makes it the duty of the preachers to enforce on our members the necessity of teaching their slaves to read the word of God, and allowing them time to attend to the public worship of God.

These regulations, like the preceding ones, surely breathe an anti-slavery spirit, and cannot, by any fair construction, be tortured into any other meaning. It may be objected, first, that these laws have not been faithfully administered; and that the action of certain annual conferences, and some acts and doings of the General Conference, have not harmonized with them. To these objections we, for the present, make no reply, not being sufficiently posted on these points to give a matured opinion; and having never claimed anything further, than that the Church, in her organic law, is opposed to slavery. It is objected, in the second place, that the Church is too obsequious to the State —the spiritual to the civil power—in regard to slavery. This objection will furnish matter for our next section.

SECTION II.

OBJECTIONS CONSIDERED:—THAT THE CHURCH IS TOO OBSEQUIOUS TO THE STATE—THE SPIRITUAL TO THE CIVIL POWER.

PURSUANT to promise, we will now examine the second objection:—"That the Church is too obsequious to the State—the spiritual to the civil power," in conforming her practice to the laws of the State, in receiving and retaining in her communion persons connected with slavery, on account of the difficulties interposed by the civil power in the way of emancipation. This, in a country like the United States, where the constitution of the general government protects the several slaveholding States in their right to hold slaves; and where the laws of such slaveholding States, to guard and protect this interest, have thrown impediments around it, rendering it almost, if not, in many instances, entirely impracticable for the citizens of those States to liberate them, by requiring the master, who may not have the means, when he would emancipate, to remove them to a free State; and rendering the slave thus emancipated, for want of such removal, liable to be taken up the next week, month, or year, and sold into perpetual bondage to a worse and more cruel master, is a grave subject, and requires our most serious attention. In examining it, we feel our want of more general reading; nevertheless, we will venture a few thoughts, showing our opinion.

From the constitution of human nature, it is manifest that man was intended for society. His weakness when born into the world, and for several years thereafter, amounting to entire helplessness; his wants, which that helplessness can in no measure, not even the least, supply, clearly indicate a social existence to have been the design of the Creator in his formation.

His love of society, seen from an early period of infancy, and which continues unabated throughout the entire period of his earthly existence, is also in proof of the above proposition.

The constitution and attachment of the sexes, one of the strongest impulsions of our nature, and which in itself leads to society, is declarative of its truth.

His capacity for mental and moral improvement, which can only be brought to any tolerable perfection in a social state, and which would be greatly retarded, if not totally defeated, on the anti-social principle, is in evidence that society is a prominent and essential principle of our nature.

Thus his incapacity to provide for, protect, and

defend himself; to indulge and gratify the social tendencies of his being; to develop his physical, mental, moral, and social powers, according to their capacity, demonstrate his formation a folly, his existence a failure, on any other principle than that of a social state.

Now if the principles and reasonings contained in the preceding remarks establish, as we think they do, the social character of human nature, government, being essential to such a state, is therefore necessary to the continued existence of the race. Ethical writers, or writers on natural law, take this view of the question, and attach such importance to the doctrine, as to tell us that man cannot exist without it; and that therefore any form of government is preferable to anarchy. The Holy Scriptures recognize this principle, not only by implication, from the historical account they give of the social state in which the race has been preserved, and the relative duties enjoined, growing out of such a state; but by positive precept, as contained in the following passages:—"Let every soul be subject unto the higher powers; for there is no power but of God. The powers that be are ordained of God." Rom. xiii, 1. "Submit yourselves to every ordinance of man for the Lord's sake: whether it be to the king, as supreme; or unto governors, as unto them that are sent by him for the punishment of evil-doers, and for the praise of them that do well." 1 Pet. ii, 13, 14. Now an institution lying thus deep at the foundation of human nature, and so clearly ascertained, certified, and authenticated, as being essential to our continued existence, cannot, when once established, be lightly regarded with impunity. And the inquiry here forces itself upon us: What is its relative position in the

Divine administration over the world? Is it subordinate to the spiritual power, or the Church, as has been claimed and practised by Popery? Or is it the supreme rule of duty, under the limitations and restrictions of the Divine law, and, as such, binding upon the conscience, regardless of the moral character of the executive, or subordinate officers of the law? This latter view seems to us to be the true state of the question; and, as will be immediately shown, is capable of the most clear and irrefragable demonstration. As just seen, man cannot exist without society; and society cannot exist without government: government, therefore, is essential to the existence of the race. The Church is only needed in the continued existence of the race: therefore, as the inevitable consequence, her subordinate position. And such seems to be the light in which it is presented in the New Testament. "Then went the Pharisees, and took counsel how they might entangle him in his talk. And they sent out unto him their disciples, with the Herodians, saying, Master, we know that thou art true, and teachest the way of God in truth, neither carest thou for any man; for thou regardest not the person of men. Tell us, therefore, What thinkest thou? Is it lawful to give tribute unto Cæsar, or not? But Jesus perceived their wickedness, and said, Why tempt ye me, ye hypocrites? Show me the tribute-money. And they brought unto him a penny. And he saith unto them, Whose is this image and superscription? They say unto him, Cæsar's. Then saith he unto them, *Render therefore unto Cæsar the things which are Cæsar's; and unto God the things that are God's.*" Matt. xxii, 15–21. "Then saith Pilate unto him, Speakest thou not unto me?

knowest thou not that I have power to crucify thee, and have power to release thee? Jesus answered, Thou couldest have no power at all against me, except it were given thee from above: therefore he that delivered me unto thee hath the greater sin." John xix, 10, 11. Other passages might be quoted, but these we think sufficient, in which the blessed Jesus, under the most public and trying circumstances, asserts the supremacy of the civil power, and that power to exist by divine appointment: "*Thou couldest have no power at all against me, except it were given thee from above.*" Therefore, whatever may have been the state of this question in the Jewish Church; and whatever arguments might thence be drawn, in regard to the elevated position of the spiritual power during its continuance; when it was superseded by the Gospel Church, its power in this particular, as well as many others peculiar to the Mosaic institution, passed away, giving place for the introduction of a kingdom not of this world. "Jesus answered, My kingdom is not of this world. If my kingdom were of this world, then would my servants fight, that I should not be delivered to the Jews: but now is my kingdom not from hence." John xviii, 36. "And one of the company said unto him, Master, speak to my brother, that he divide the inheritance with me. And he said unto him, Man, who made me a judge or a divider over you?" Luke xii, 13, 14. "And in the days of these kings shall the God of heaven set up a kingdom, which shall never be destroyed: and the kingdom shall not be left to other people, but it shall break in pieces and consume all these kingdoms, and it shall stand forever," Dan. ii, 44; that is, it shall not be blended with the secular or civil power, as was the Jewish Church. Accordingly we find, in the teaching and example of Christ and the apostles, a recognition of the separation of the Church and State, Luke xii, 14; and also of the supremacy of the civil power in all the duties of civil or organized society. Matt. xvii, 24–27; Luke xx, 25; Rom. xiii, 1–7; Tit. iii, 1; and 1 Pet. ii, 13, 14. Therefore we conclude, that whatever we, as individual members of the Church, and as subjects of the civil power, may regard as our duty toward the government under which we live, it is not competent for the Church, in her organized capacity, to array herself against the powers that be, or any of the civil duties legitimately growing out of the constitution under which we live, when they do not conflict with the law of God. If the constitution in its essential principles is good, and their practical tendency in detail is to secure the common welfare, it is our solemn duty, as citizens and as Christians, to support it, and obey all its clearly ascertained and properly accredited duties. For this we are responsible, not only as citizens and subjects of the civil government, by the laws of the state in which we live; but as Christians, by the more weighty consideration that these civil administrations are taken into the Divine administration, and that the God and Judge of all, who "ordained the powers that be," will, in the final judgment, hold us responsible for any neglect of duty to the State.

If corruptions or abuses, tending to subvert the ends of good government, have by any means crept into an administration carried on under a constitution in itself good, it is then our duty, as citizens and as Christians, by petition, and all other peaceful measures provided under the constitution, to seek to have such corruptions or abuses reformed. If the constitution be in itself a bad one, and the operation of its essential or accidental principles tend to the common injury, or the injury of any portion of the community, it then becomes our duty, both as citizens and Christians, to take the proper steps to have it entirely annulled, altered, or amended, as will best secure the universal good.

Should it be inquired, Has the Church, in her organized capacity, nothing to do in this business—no part to act beyond the instruction of mankind in the principles and duties of Christianity, and building up believers in the faith of the gospel? We answer, this is her direct and appropriate work—the mission God has given her to a sin-ruined world. In this, as her principal, her first great business, she is to be actively, vigilantly, and untiringly engaged. "Christ crucified, the power of God and the wisdom of God," and, we will add, the goodness of God and the justice of God, is, according to the Scriptures, to be the all-absorbing theme—the moral lever by which to move the world, and move it in the right direction. All others are inefficient, as principles of reforming power, in the sense in which she is directly charged with the world's reformation.

True, the wide range of topics contained in the gospel, embracing every principle important to the happiness of man, as a civil, social, and moral being, presents various subjects of interest for the common good;—such as the great doctrine of human rights, the common brotherhood of man, the peace and temperance movements, &c.—which should claim the attention of the Church, to elaborate and enforce them upon the attention and practice of the world; and so far as she fails in giving due prominence to all such useful lessons of instruction, she is recreant to her duty in the great commission received from her Lord. But this is to be done by moral suasion; or the clear exhibition of these principles, in their practical utility and beneficial results; and not by arraying the Church against the government; nor yet by excluding from her fellowship persons who, by the operation of a civil power they did not personally create, and cannot personally control, are involved in a great evil; which, in its general character and consequences—aside from the circumstances above named—may be a great sin, without an express or clearly implied warrant from the word of God.

It may be objected here, that, numerically, the individual members of the Church have, as citizens of the State, the control of the ballot-box; and, failing to use it, do, as Christian citizens, become responsible for the evil; and therefore the Church would now be justified in their exclusion from her pale, and making it in future a bar to communion. This objection, we think, is not well founded, not being sustained by the facts in the case, the statistics of the Church showing that the majority of the citizens of the State are not members of the Church; and therefore, as Christian citizens, they are in the minority, and have not the control of the civil power.

But allowing, for the sake of argument, that they have the numerical strength by which to control the civil power; and having failed to use it, is it not the duty of the Church to excommunicate them? Should we grant this, still it does not follow that the Church would have the right to refuse admission to other applicants for membership connected with the evil, because the individual members of the Church have, as citizens of the State, failed to do their duty.

But it is further objected, that the professing portion of the community, with their influence, that is, the numbers they could bring with them to the ballot-box, have the numerical strength to control the civil power; and not having done so, therefore it is the duty of the Church, so far as the membership who are connected with the evil is concerned, to exclude them; and why not those unconnected with the evil? who, in respect to the evil, have failed to do their duty at the ballot-box; and thus well-nigh unchurch the Church?

But if we should, for the sake of argument, admit this also; still the former difficulty occurs in all its force, and she therefore remains liable to a connexion with the evil.

We, however, doubt the correctness of this last objection; the moral sentiment of the age is not sufficiently matured to sustain it. And you ask where lies the blame in this matter? Possibly in different directions; partly in the weakness and slowness of the human mind—enervated and clouded by sin—to discover, examine, comprehend, and carry out, in their practical bearings, those great principles which are to work this moral improvement;—and partly on the Church, for not having, as the light of the world, furnished the necessary amount of instruction to form such moral sentiment. But she cannot now consistently atone for past delinquency, by excluding and debarring from her pale those who, by her neglect, are not qualified for this lofty range of moral duty. Now admitting the premises in this argument, namely, the separation of the Church from the State, and the supremacy of the civil power; the conclusion, as it seems to us, is inevitable, that it is not competent for the Church, under the present condition of organized society, to make the simple act of slaveholding, aside from the abuses of the system, a bar to Christian fellowship. It would be a violation of the great principle laid down in Scripture, "that it is required according to what a man hath, and not according to what he hath not." Thus, we think, by a simple course of obvious reasoning, we have arrived at the conclusion, so far as this view of the subject is concerned, that the Church is not pro-slavery.

This is a subject, at this particular juncture, of superlative importance to the American Church. And the writer feels exceedingly solicitous to be correct in the views he may entertain and advance on a question so momentous. And if, by any species of illusion, he has so far imposed upon his own understanding as to lead him from the path of truth, he is not aware of it; and on being convinced—not by hard words, but by hard arguments—that he is in error, he will immediately renounce it.

But it is claimed, on the principles here laid down—the separation of the Church and State, and the supremacy of the civil power—that the Church would be bound to admit to her communion highwaymen, adulterers, drunkards, &c., if such practices were authorized by the laws of the State. The examination of this objection will form the subject-matter of our next section.

SECTION III.

OBJECTIONS CONSIDERED.—THAT THE SAME PRINCIPLES THAT RECEIVE SLAVEHOLDERS INTO THE CHURCH, REQUIRE THE RECEPTION OF HIGHWAYMEN, ADULTERERS, AND MURDERERS.

In conformity with our promise, we will now examine the above objection—that the Church being subordinate to the State, &c. This objection, frequently and clamorously urged by many, may, on first sight, appear not only formidable, but really insurmountable. We are not so far intimidated by its supposed Alpine strength, as to be deterred from approaching it with the lamp of reason and the light of truth, to examine its base, structure, and proportions, and ascertain whether there is not more sand than rock, more speciousness than solidity about it.

And, first; when we look fairly at it, there appears on its face what logicians call "a begging of the question;" it being assumed that the laws of the State do authorize all these and like practices, which is not the fact with regard to either or any of them. For they are all taken and held in law to be offences against the State; and all persons so offending are, on conviction thereof, liable to the penalties of the law. The objection thus far is only sand.

But it may be inquired, Do not the laws of the State license houses of drunkenness and debauchery? Facts compel us, in the nineteenth century, to answer, to our great reproach, that such is the law. But granting this, it does not follow that persons guilty of these practices are, on application, to be received into the Church; for this plain and sufficient reason—the license laws merely allow, or authorize, such houses; but do not compel any person, or persons, to keep them; much less do they compel any man, woman, or child, in all the land, to frequent them, and revel in their midnight orgies of intemperance and uncleanness. Whereas the laws of the State, with regard to slavery, do compel a man to become a slaveholder or owner. For instance; the laws of many of the slaveholding States run thus: My father may be the owner of one hundred slaves; he is about to die: by his last will and testament he leaves those slaves to me. Thus, by the strong arm of the law, I am made a slaveholder, possibly without my knowledge or consent. For we believe it is the practice, to some extent, for wills to be made privately; the heirs knowing little or nothing about their contents. Or suppose he dies without a will, and that I am his only heir, or one among many, as the case may be; by the law of the State in this case also, I become the owner of slaves, whether I will or not. So that the cases are not parallel in any rational view we can take of them; and the objection, therefore, totally fails; it being all sand and show, having no rock or solidity about it.

But in this connexion it may be well to look at the subject in another direction. It is urged, if the law has forced me into slavery, I can liberate the slaves, and thus secure their freedom. Should we allow this, for the sake of argument, it does not help the objection an iota. For it does not show how I may keep out of the difficulty or connexion; but how I may get out when once involved.

And besides, my liberating them is somewhat problematical. I can do it, having the means to remove them to a free State; otherwise my doing so may not secure their freedom; they being liable, for the want of such removal, to be taken up, and sold the next week, or month, or year, into perpetual bondage, and myself in the mean while responsible for their support and good behaviour.

Another evil, and one among the greatest belonging to the whole system of American slavery, and for which it is so justly denounced, must be inflicted by the liberation and indiscriminate removal of the slaves to a free State;—the separation of husband and wife, parents and children. For it is a well-known truth, that the slaves belonging to different masters are intermarried for miles around on the different plantations, in the various sections of country where they live. So that, if we would liberate and remove them to a free State, unless it was a unanimous or universal thing, which is not to be expected, and is not contemplated by the measures we oppose, we should separate husband and wife; and thus sin against God, by putting asunder that which he has joined together; or against the slaves, should we not remove them, by placing them in circumstances where their condition may be worsted. For it is fairly to be presumed, that the man who would liberate them, could he do it without inflicting a greater injury than to retain them, would be more likely to sympathize with, and treat them humanely and kindly, than the human shark, who would buy them back into slavery or bondage, under the provisions of the law, when thus emancipated. So that, all things considered, the policy of liberating them under the circumstances supposed, which do in fact exist in some of the Southern States, is questionable, on the great principle laid down in the golden rule: "Therefore all things whatsoever ye would that men should do to you, do ye even so to them."

But to place the objection in its strongest light,

namely: suppose the laws of the State, as nearly as the nature of the case will allow, coerced men into highway robbery, adultery, drunkenness, &c., just as we have shown they do coerce men into slavery; would not the Church be under the same obligation to receive the highwayman, adulterer, or drunkard, that she would be to receive a slaveholder? We answer, No! believing we are sustained by the following reason: The slaves were slaves, in the eye and by the force of law, to all intents and purposes, before they came into my possession; and without any act of mine to set up, or establish a claim; or should I deny, or refuse all claim or right in them, still, by the force of law, they are my property. There is no alternative. I have no volition in the case. Moral principle is not involved; for I have transgressed no law, human or divine. I, therefore, am not guilty; and, consequently, have no cause of repentance, so far as my connexion with slavery is concerned. But this reasoning will not apply to the highwayman, adulterer, or drunkard. True, the law coercing them to the commission of robbery, adultery, drunkenness, &c., may have existed before they were born; consequently without their agency. But the doing these acts in obedience to the laws implies volition. It may be a constrained volition, wrought up by the penal sanctions of the law; still it is volition. They might have chosen otherwise; and ought to have so chosen, at all hazards; because a higher authority has said, "Thou shalt not kill, thou shalt not steal, thou shalt not commit adultery;" and choosing to obey man rather than God, they are guilty; moral turpitude attaches to them by their own act of obedience to human authority, in despite of the authority of

God, who says, "Be not afraid of them that kill the body, and after that have no more that they can do. But fear Him which, after he hath killed, hath power to cast into hell; yea, I say unto you, fear him." Thus, by a simple course of obvious (not to say irrefutable) reasoning, we have routed this objection, till there is nothing of it left. Other arguments are not wanting, were they necessary; but "I speak as to wise men, judge ye what I say."

But it is claimed that all the slavery in the United States is man-stealing—therefore wicked, and, by consequence, a bar to church-fellowship. The Rev. Edward Smith, in our discussion in Senecaville, (which grew out of the resolution before named,) staked the whole issue on this view of the question. We will look at it a little, and see if it will stand the test of rational investigation. If the major proposition in this argument is true, the minor logically follows; and the conclusion is inevitable. For man-stealing, according to the Scriptures, is one of the highest crimes a man can commit against his fellow-man; and he who is guilty, without repentance and restitution, if in his power, deserves death, rather than a place in the Church of God. But the question here arises, is the proposition true? Is all the slavery in the United States man-stealing? We think we have, in the preceding remarks, clearly demonstrated the utter fallacy of this proposition; both as to the manner of our connexion with it, and the circumstances by, and under which, that connexion is continued. By proving, first, that we had no volition in said connexion; and, in the second place, that under the circumstances, we may either be compelled to retain them in slavery, or rationally conclude, all things considered, that it is best for the slaves themselves not to liberate them.

That the original act by which this Heaven-insulting and man-degrading business was commenced, and is perpetuated, is man-stealing, is not denied. But we are not now considering the question in its incipiency, or first aggressions, but as an element of organized society,—a part and parcel of the civil regulations of the State, by which the relation is formed, and the duties and responsibilities of the parties thereto are detailed and enforced.

And, if we are not mistaken, the Scriptures make this distinction. When they speak of man-stealing, they represent the act as exceedingly flagitious, and denounce death as the punishment of the offender. "He that stealeth a man and selleth him, or if he be found in his hand, he shall surely be put to death." Exod. xxi, 16; Deut. xxiv, 7.

But when they speak of slavery as a civil relation, established in the State, as in Eph. vi, 5, 9; Col. iii, 22, 25, and iv, 1; 1 Tim. vi, 1, 2, &c.; they enjoin a kind, humane, and Christian conduct on the part of the masters toward their servants or slaves; and faithfulness on the part of servants toward their masters, in all their relative duties.

But it is objected, that the servitude spoken of in these pages is not slavery. We answer: probably, so far as the manner in which men become slaveholders is concerned, it is full two-thirds, or three-fourths, of all the slavery in the United States; and so far as the Church is concerned, it is a rational conclusion, that still a greater proportion of them become slaveholders in this way. To what extent the circumstances above alluded to, and others of some force that might be stated, operate to continue them in the relation of masters, we are not prepared to say; but we are fairly entitled to the conclusion, that they operate to a considerable extent, especially so far as the Church is concerned.

Now in the sense in which slavery is discussed in these pages—for we speak not of it as a whole—we wish it distinctly understood, that we are not speaking of the right of one man to kidnip or steal another, and thus reduce him from a state of freedom to a state of bondage; nor whether the laws that create, regulate, and perpetuate it, are righteous and just laws; nor whether it is right to treat slaves cruelly and brutally; nor yet whether slavery as a system, as it exists in several of the slaveholding States, under the protection of the General Government, is right;—but of slavery as a part and parcel of the political and civil regulations of the State; descending to, and continuing with us, by the force of law, and the circumstances above noted, which that law throws around it. We say slavery, in this sense, to those thus connected with it, is not a sin. They have violated no law in becoming connected with it; and may be governed by considerations of mercy to the slave, in continuing that connexion. Therefore, the resolution of the Georgia, and some other southern annual conference, "that slavery is not a moral evil," so far as this particular view of the subject is concerned, is true.

And we might go further, and say, the buying or selling them, as an act of mercy to the slaves, is not a moral evil. Do not be startled, gentle reader, at the apparent boldness of this position; hear us candidly and patiently through, and we think we shall prove to your satisfaction that the truth lies in this direction.

For instance: a slave is in the hands of a cruel, iron-hearted master, who abuses him in a most severe and brutal manner, denying him all religious privileges, etc. Now, suppose yourself not able to purchase such a one, and liberate him; but could make arrangements to purchase, by retaining the services of the person thus bought; would you not be doing an act of mercy, in the sight of heaven and earth, toward that slave, if, after having bought him, you treated him with humanity and Christian kindness, allowing his religious privileges, and instructing him in the way of salvation? The question is not, could not more have been done for him? This may be granted; but, having done all you were able to do, have you sinned against God or man by so doing? We answer, most unhesitatingly, No!

But then it is inquired as to selling, as an act of mercy. We answer on this wise: You or I may own a man; some other neighbour may own his wife. She, under the heart-rending workings of the system, may be sold out of the neighbourhood into a more or less distant part. Suppose we had an opportunity of selling the husband into the same neighbourhood; where, in all other matters, he would fare equally well, or better than with us, and enjoy the company of his wife and family into the bargain; would we not be doing him a kindness by selling him? The question is not here, again, have we done the best that might be done? But, supposing we could do no better for him; have we done wickedly in selling him into the hands of another master, where, all things else being equal, or better, he can enjoy the additional happiness of his wife and children? Religion, reason, humanity, and common sense, answer No! God, in the judgment at the last day, will approve the act: "Inasmuch as ye have done it unto one of the least of these my brethren, ye have done it unto me." The case, however, should be clearly and fully covered by the rule. The "pride of life," or the love of ambition or ease, should be vigilantly watched and guarded; lest our own gratification and convenience, regardless of the good of the servant, lead us astray from the principle laid down. And in view of such liability, it would be the most prudent course to have the least to do with it that we possibly can; and never, on any terms, touch, taste, or handle, in a case involved in any degree of doubt or uncertainty: "For he that doubteth is damned if he eat."

All other traffic in slaves is essential wickedness; and the monster in human form who deals in the souls and bodies of men for the sake of gain, deserves the execration of all mankind. Worse! To be delivered over to Heaven's bangman, and lashed naked all around the horizon of heaven's circumference. Worse! To be shut up in the dominions of old Apollyon,—handed over to the care of his Satanic majesty, who will assign him, if not a comfortable and honourable place, the very best accommodations in all the infernal regions, in the shape of close and hot quarters. And doubtless, if he could disentangle himself from those chains of darkness, in which he is reserved unto the judgment of the great day,—fearing a rivalship in the reign of Pandemonium, in the character of this aspiring fiend, in the shape of humanity,—a sight over which all heaven weeps, and hell,—profoundest hell, grows pale with consternation,—he would effectually and eternally secure him against further encroachments on the rights of his throne.

If he can, may God have mercy on these, the devil's nearest relations, with all their aiders and abettors ;—and especially all those who breed human beings for market, as honest people do cattle, and horses, and other descriptions of stock.

SECTION IV.

OBJECTION CONSIDERED—THAT THE SAME PRINCIPLE THAT RECEIVES SLAVE-HOLDERS INTO THE CHURCH, REQUIRES THE RECEPTION OF THE POLYGAMIST.

Since writing out our thoughts on slavery, as connected with the moral and providential government of God ; a friend to whom we submitted them for critical observation, and whose judgment is entitled to respect, offered verbally, if our memory serves us right, the following objection : That the Polygamist, on a profession of faith in Christ, is just as eligible to church-membership as a man in the slavery relation, on a like profession of faith. Shortly subsequent to our friend's objection, another friend placed in our hands the works of Doctor Channing on slavery, whose views, if not in exact accordance with the above objection, would tend very much to strengthen such objections in the minds of those who, prior to their having read the Doctor's works, had embraced it. The difference, however, between them, as it appears to us, would be this : our friend, in defiance of existing civil authority, and the teaching of the Scriptures, would entirely exclude the relation from the Church. The Doctor would acknowledge the authority of the teaching of the Scriptures, and, as we think, the relation as being compatible with a creditable profession of Christianity; but at the same time oppose the essential rightfulness of slavery. For he says, "Of what avail are a few texts, which were designed for local and temporary use, when urged against the vital, essential spirit, and plainest precepts of our religion?" In regard to the temporary character of the regulation of slavery as taught in the Scriptures, we are pleased to find the views we have offered on this aspect of the question sustained by so respectable authority. We think, however, that on the whole there is some little confusion of thought in the Doctor's views on this subject. In answer to the following argument in favour of slavery, viz., "Slavery, it is said, is allowed in the Old Testament, and not condemned in the New; Paul commands slaves to obey; he commands masters not to release their slaves, but to treat them justly. Therefore slavery is right, is sanctified by God's word:"—he says, in vol. ii, page 99, "This reasoning proves too much. If usages sanctioned in the Old Testament, and not forbidden in the New, are right, then our moral code will undergo a sad deterioration. Polygamy was allowed to the Israelites, was the practice of the holiest men, and was common and licensed in the age of the apostles. But the apostles nowhere condemn it, nor was the renunciation of it made an essential condition of admission into the Christian Church. It is true, that in one passage Christ has condemned it by implication. But is not slavery condemned by stronger implication, in the many passages which make the new religion to consist in serving one another, and in doing to others what we would they should do to ourselves? Why may not Scripture be used to stock our houses with wives as well as slaves?" If by this language we are to understand the Doctor as placing polygamy and slavery in the same category, as to original right, there is no controversy between us. For with him, as the reader has seen, and will further see in the sequel, we do not believe in the essential rightfulness of slavery. But if we are to understand him, as my friend's objection supposes, that in the teaching of the New Testament the same tolerance is lent to the practice of polygamy that is lent to the practice of slavery, we must, for the following reasons, beg leave to dissent from both their views. And first: from the teaching of Christ and the apostles, it is obvious beyond controversy that a man is restricted to one wife, and a woman to one husband, at a time. Jesus says, "For this cause shall a man leave his father and mother, and shall cleave unto his wife: and they twain shall be one flesh." Matt. xix, 5. And Paul says, "Nevertheless let every man have his own wife, and let every woman have her own husband." 1 Cor. vii, 2. "For this cause shall a man leave his father and mother, and shall be joined unto his wife, and they two shall be one flesh. And nevertheless let every one of you in particular so love his wife even as himself, and the wife see that she reverence her husband." Eph. v, 31, 33. In 1 Tim. iii, 2, 12, as also in Titus i, 6, the apostle, speaking of the qualifications of bishops and deacons, says, "they must be the husband of one wife." That is, we suppose, it was lawful for them to have one wife,—and but one,—at the same time. So that nothing can be more plain and clear than that it is the Divine will that every son of Adam should have a daughter of Eve, and *vice versa.*

And this view of the subject is very much strengthened by all that catalogue of Scriptures which allows sexual intercourse only in lawful wedlock; and invariably restricts it under the fearful penalty of the Divine displeasure, both here and hereafter, to the one lawful wife, or husband. So that there is no room for inference that the gospel dispensation, under any circumstances, recognizes or tolerates the lawfulness of polygamy, or a plurality of wives.

For, second: While, as we have seen and proved by various passages of Scripture, and which might have been greatly multiplied, both from the Gospels and the Epistles, that it is according to the laws of Christianity for a man to have one wife, there is not the most distant intimation to be found in the New Testament that it will meet the Divine forbearance or tolerance that we have a plurality of wives or husbands,—that is, more than one at a time. And hence all approbatory allusions to the conjugal state in the New Testament are restricted to the husband of one wife, or the wife of one husband.

True, it may be argued that, in the Epistles to Timothy and Titus, in the language above quoted, where the bishops and deacons are restricted to one wife, by implication a plurality of wives would be allowable, to such as were not in the pastoral office. Should we for the sake of argument concede this, it would necessarily carry with it the following very embarrassing difficulty: that drunkenness, and all the other bad traits of character there enumerated and condemned, would be no objection to the Christian character of those not in the pastoral office; which would be fatal to the argument.

But another discrimination, of striking importance to

the correct understanding of the points of disagreement in which these two questions are presented in the New Testament, is that as above stated, while they nowhere intimate that polygamy would be allowed or tolerated, and hence give no instructions for the regulation of a plurality of wives, or more than one at a time. They do, according to the Doctor's own acknowledgment, distinctly recognize and tolerate the relation of slavery, as a temporary regulation, and give those instructions for its government which were calculated to make the best of it under the circumstances; and which, on his acknowledgment, were in force up to the time of his writing the work from which we quote; for he not only admits, but lauds, the private virtue and Christian love of those in the relation. On page 54, he says: "Absolute monarchy is still a scourge, though among despots there have been good men. It is possible to abhor and oppose bad institutions, and yet to abstain from indiscriminate condemnation of those who cling to them, and even to see in their ranks greater virtue than in ourselves. It is true, and ought to be cheerfully acknowledged, that in the slaveholding States may be found some of the greatest names of our history, and, what is still more important, bright examples of private virtue and Christian love." Now how, in view of all these facts, it can be claimed by the Doctor that polygamy and slavery stand precisely on the same footing; and by our friend, that polygamy is just as eligible to church-fellowship as the slavery relation, we are at an utter loss to conceive. In either case, to make good their respective positions, they should give us the same unequivocal Scriptural laws, on the authority of the New Testament, to govern polygamy in the Church, that are given for this purpose to govern the relation of slavery; or otherwise wholly disprove the applicability of those passages to the slavery relation that are claimed in its support. This the Doctor does not attempt; but unhesitatingly admits their applicability and force temporarily, as before stated. And we think our friend will not stake his reputation for critical authority against the learning of the Church and of the world. And we think, instead of finding a like amount of Scriptural authority to govern polygamy in the Church that is found to govern the relation of slavery, as a temporary regulation, there cannot, as before stated, be found one single passage that, by any torturing, can be made to look to its recognition and regulation in the Church. And further, if polygamy, like slavery, was authorized by existing civil laws, and was to any considerable extent the practice of the country, the facts already stated—first, that it is the doctrine of the New Testament that a man shall have but one wife at the same time; and, secondly, that there is not in all the New Testament the most distant approbatory allusion to, or tolerant recognition of, the practice of polygamy—place the action of the Church on very distinct and entirely different grounds. In the case of polygamy, be the civil authority for or against it—law or no law—all we can learn from the New Testament respecting it, is clearly and unequivocally against it, as an element of Church organization; whereas, the relation of slavery, on the teaching of the New Testament, as expounded by the best critical and literary lights the Church and the world have produced, was, in the days of the apostles, taken into the Church, and suitable directions given for its regulation, as an element of religious society. Therefore the cases are not in agreement; and the argument that will sustain the action of the Church in the one case, affords no plea whatever in the other. And further, the principle of volition or agency involved in the case of the highwayman, adulterer, or drunkard, before alluded to, applies, in all its force, to the polygamist.

NOTE. On reading this section to our friend above alluded to, he informed us, that he did not intend to be understood as saying, that the cases were presented in the same light in the New Testament. Having, however, frequently heard the argument used by others, we insert the article.

SECTION V.

THE RELATION OF SLAVERY AS TAUGHT IN THE OLD TESTAMENT.

THE Scriptures teach us that God is not careless of the conduct of his rational creatures; that such is the essential goodness and rectitude of his nature, that he has an infinite pleasure in our doing right, and is always displeased with us when we do wrong. Right and wrong, or righteousness and wickedness, are relative terms, having respect to some rule or law by which the moral quality of actions or relations is determined. That rule or law is the word of God—the Scriptures of the Old and New Testaments; which profess to be, and are received by all Christians as, a revelation from heaven, for the instruction of mankind in the principles and practice of moral duty.

And when we consider the ignorance and wants of the world, together with the essential character of the Author of the Bible, as a God of wisdom, truth, and goodness, as we might naturally expect, there is a fulness of instruction, embracing everything important for us to know, to guide us into all truth, in all the various relations and duties of the present life. On the verity of this proposition, we presume there is no disagreement among Christians. And infidels have done homage to the Scriptures, by acknowledging and testifying to the sublimity and super-excellence of their moral teachings. The difficulty is not as to the verity of what they teach, and its paramount obligation on mankind as a rule of duty, but what they teach—what is their meaning on this, that, or the other subject. The most serious and heated, not to say angry and bloody controversies, have frequently grown out of mere differences of opinion as to what they teach: not so much, however, on questions of moral duty, as on other notions and opinions that are not really essential to religion. Happily for the world, the reign of ignorance and passion is fast passing away; while reason and truth are asserting and maintaining empire, to the honour of human nature, and the glory of Christianity. So that on questions indifferent, we more generally agree to disagree; and conduct our disputations involving more essential points, with a marked spirit of courtesy and forbearance, as compared with former ages of the Church. Exceptions to the rule are not of so frequent occurrence as formerly; and, in Protestant Christendom, appear, so far as we are posted on the subject, to be mainly confined to the partisans taking different, or apparently different positions on the slavery question;

which we acknowledge to be an exciting question, and, without great precaution, liable to lead to different conclusions in our search after the truth; and the grounds of difference in those conclusions may, as we think, be summed up in the following considerations:—

First: Our education, or the preconceived opinions we bring with us to the Bible, if we examine it at all; by which its teachings are prejudged, and made to speak a language in unison with such education or opinion, either for or against, as the case may be;—a state of mind, at all times, under all circumstances, and on all subjects, unfavourable to the eliciting and ascertainment of truth. Second: Views hastily drawn from a partial examination of the Scriptures, or from certain general principles laid down in the Bible, with which, it is believed, and confidently asserted, the slavery relation cannot be reconciled.

Now, while it is a rational conclusion, that a man, who brings his preconceived opinions to the Bible for support, or who hastily and partially examines the Scriptures on this or any other subject, may arrive at erroneous opinions; it may be readily admitted, that general principles may be a safe guide to conduct us to proper conclusions on any given subject, in the absence of specific law. But when we have the direct teaching of the Scriptures with regard to such subject, it becomes our duty to seek the best method of explaining and harmonizing what may seem contradictory; rather than array Scripture against Scripture, and thus make the word of God contradict itself. Or if the seeming or apparent difficulty is above our comprehension, it would be more modest and becoming in us, to set it down to our want of capacity to grasp the vastness of his plans of government and providence;—concluding with the Psalmist, that to us "clouds and darkness" may be round about an administration, embracing all worlds, sweeping over all time, and extending through all eternity; but rejoicing at the same time to know, that God sits above the clouds, and above the darkness, and, with calm and unruffled dignity, surveys the harmonious workings of all its parts, and its final tendency to secure the common and greatest good of all his creatures.

To the law and testimony, as the ultimate standard of appeal for the settlement of this question. For whatever position we may take, if it does not accord with, and cannot be sustained by, their teachings, it has not truth for its foundation.

We will first call attention to the Old Testament Scriptures. And the question here arises, Does the teaching of that book recognize the relation of one man, as the servant and slave of another; and the master or owner as having a right of property in such servant or slave?

In Genesis xvii, 12, 13, where the rite of circumcision is instituted and enjoined, Abraham is commanded to circumcise every man-child eight days old, born in his house or bought with his money. Now here appear to be two classes of dependents or servants,—one a household servant, the other his slave, bought with his money. For we find in the 23d verse, that Abraham took Ishmael, his son, and all that were born in his house, and bought with his money, every male that was among them, and circumcised them on the self-same day as God had said unto him. So that there were two classes independent of his family direct; one of which was his property, having been bought with his money.

In the 21st chapter of the Book of Exodus, where sundry laws are given respecting men-servants, we find the relation and property principle not only stated, but distinctly recognized as a part and parcel of the political regulations by which Jehovah intended to govern the Jewish nation, and those of the heathen nations round about, who became incorporated with them. The chapter opens with these remarkable words: "Now these are the judgments which thou shalt set before them." And those relating to the question under consideration, found in the 20th and 21st verses, are as follows: "And if a man smite his servant, or his maid, with a rod, and he die under his hand, he shall surely be punished. Notwithstanding, if he continue (live) a day or two, he shall not be punished; for he is his money." In examining the Jewish law, the intelligent reader will observe the change in the penal sanctions, or punishment, by which the violation of these civil or political regulations are visited.

"He that smiteth a man, so that he die, shall surely be put to death."

"If a man come presumptuously upon his neighbour, to slay him with guile,"—he is to die.

"And he that smiteth his father or his mother, shall be surely put to death."

"And he that stealeth a man and selleth him, or if he be found in his hand, he shall surely be put to death."

But if he smite his servant, so that he die under his hand, he is to be punished; should he live a day or two, and then die, he is not liable to any punishment;

the law presuming some other agency as the cause of his death, than the correction administered by the master.

It is to this principle in the political constitution, or civil regulations, of the Jewish government, relative to the correction of servants, that the laws of many, if not of all the slaveholding States, on this subject, are to be traced. This is the clue to their origin, as appears from their close agreement in some of their details; and also from the well-known fact, that all the governments of civilized and Christian nations have drawn largely on the principles of civil polity laid down in the Jewish Scriptures.

We have not called up this case for the purpose of justifying, in this age of the world, and in a country where Christianity and civilization have received their strongest development, either the inhumanity of the laws for the correction or punishment of servants or slaves, or the protection of the master in his worse than brutal cruelty in the punishment often inflicted. But, first, for the information of those who may have no knowledge of this Jewish precedent, from which these laws are derived. And, second, to show the confidence these States may have in the correctness of their political and civil regulations, as being manifestly drawn, in this particular, from this precedent in the Jewish law;—hoping thereby to soften, in some degree, the asperity generally felt, and the bitterness of invective often indulged, in the expression of our sentiments and feelings on this very grave question; and so far, and no farther, than may be in accordance with truth in the premises, stir up a feeling of sympathy, that will lead us to make due allowance for the overawing tendency of authority drawn from that source; and to expostulate with them as rational and accountable beings, in the spirit of candour; and thus endeavour to show them, that interest and duty conspire to require them, in this matter, to put away the evil of their doings.

In the twenty-fifth chapter of the book of Leviticus, commencing at the thirty-ninth verse, the bond-servant or slavery relation, and property-principle, is again brought into notice, in a way, and under circumstances, that mark its distinction from hired service or bond-service, as in the case of apprenticeship. "And if thy brother that dwelleth by thee be waxen poor, and be sold unto thee, thou shalt not compel him to serve as a bond-servant; but as a hired servant, and as a sojourner, he shall be with thee, and shall serve thee unto the year of jubilee. And then shall he depart from thee, both he and his children with him, and shall return unto his own family, and unto the possession of his fathers shall he return. For they are my servants which I brought forth out of the land of Egypt; they shall not be sold as bondmen. Thou shalt not rule over them with rigour, but shalt fear thy God. Both thy bond-men and bond-maids, which thou shalt have, shall be of the heathen that are round about you; of them shall ye buy bond-men and bond-maids. Moreover, of the children of the strangers that do sojourn among you, of them shall ye buy, and of their families that are with you, which they begat in your land; and they shall be your possession, and ye shall take them as an inheritance for your children after you, to inherit them for a possession; they shall be your bond-men forever; but over your brethren, the children of Israel, ye shall not rule one over another with rigour."

It will be seen by the intelligent reader, that there is quite a difference made between the Jewish servant and the heathen servant; or those that were made servants of the families of the strangers that dwelt among them. With regard to Jewish servants, they were not to be ruled over with rigour by an Israelite, nor were they to suffer a sojourner or stranger to rule over one of their brethren with rigour in their sight. And in the hands of either Jew or sojourner, he was to be considered and treated as a hired servant, and not as a bondsman; and could not be retained in servitude in the hands of his brother longer than seven years, (Exod. xxi, 2,) unless by the voluntary agreement of the parties. And that there might be no deception or imposition practised in the matter, all such cases were examined in the most public and solemn manner, and ratified by a simple, but most significant rite,—the boring the ear with an awl at the door-post, which signified, says Clarke, his attachment to the house and family of his master, and his readiness to hear and obey punctually all his master's orders. Exod. xxi, 56.

There seems to be a difference as to the length of time he might have to serve a stranger or sojourner, should he fall into the hands of such a one,—till the year of jubilee, which occurred every fiftieth year. This liability, however, was contingent. If himself or his friends were not able to redeem him, he had to remain till the year of jubilee. If either were able, he could be redeemed at any time. There was no such provision in behalf of the other servants, bought of the heathen or of the families of strangers that dwelt among them. They were to be bond-servants to them and their children forever, and, as such, liable, in that capacity, to needful correction.

Another thought here in this connexion, and of some importance in establishing the property principle, is found in the fourth verse of the twenty-first chapter of Exodus; where the children of the bond mother are said to partake of her condition, though the father may be entitled to his liberty.

Now, that this general view of this grave question may not be disregarded and set aside as a thing of naught, it ought, or should be remembered, that the Almighty and allwise God personally delivered these several laws to Abraham and Moses; as the reader will find by referring to the several books, chapters, and verses, from which we have quoted. And it is, or should be, enough for man to know that God has spoken, to reverence his authority.

SECTION VI.

THE RELATION OF SLAVERY, AS TAUGHT IN THE NEW TESTAMENT.

Having cursorily examined the Old Testament Scriptures on this subject, we will proceed in the next place to call attention to what is said about it in the New; and passing over all merely incidental allusions, we will examine those passages that bear directly on the question.

In 1 Cor. chap. vii, the apostle, when advising or enjoining persons in the various conditions of life to be content with the allotments of Providence, gives this general direction: "Let every man abide in the same calling wherein he was called." And then, by way of particularizing, he says, "Art thou called being a servant? care not for it; but if thou mayest be made free, use it rather. For he that is called in the Lord, being a servant, is the Lord's free man: likewise also he that is called, being free, is Christ's servant." This language is spoken of a person in a state of bondage, or slavery. Such is conceded to be its meaning, even by some of the most ultra abolitionists. Some, however, deny this interpretation; claiming that it relates to hired service or apprenticeship; for whose sake, as to its true import, we will offer some thoughts by way of criticism, and which appear to us sufficient to settle the question. The language used is such as cannot be rationally understood of hired service or apprenticeship: "If thou mayest be made free," clearly implying the possibility that the persons addressed or spoken to may never obtain their liberty or freedom. And, as all know that hired labourers or apprentices, according to the laws governing those relations, do, at a stipulated time, obtain their freedom, the language here used can, by no torturing, be made to apply to such cases. But moreover, such a construction would involve the very serious difficulty that the apostle was endeavouring to unsettle those very useful and necessary relations of society. For it is clear, from the face of the passage, that a state of freedom from their legal term of employment or servitude was better for them, and, as such, to be preferred and sought. Now, not to say anything of the effect of such teaching upon the infant kingdom of our Lord Jesus Christ in the world, which, doubtless, must have been most disastrous, how would the apostle appear before an intelligent universe, as a man of sound, discriminating judgment? It places him in a most unenviable predicament as a man of sense, and must, therefore, if it have any meaning at all, and we can form any just conceptions of the ideas language is designed to convey, relate to a state of slavery. There is no getting away from this conclusion.

The next passages found in the New Testament to which we shall call attention are, Eph. vi, 5–8: "Servants, be obedient to them that are your masters according to the flesh, with fear and trembling, in singleness of your heart, as unto Christ; not with eye-service, as men-pleasers; but as the servants of Christ, doing the will of God from the heart; with good-will doing service, as to the Lord, and not to men: knowing that whatsoever good thing any man doeth, the same shall he receive of the Lord, whether he be bond or free." Col. iii, 22: "Servants, obey in all things your masters according to the flesh; not with eye-service, as men-pleasers; but in singleness of heart, fearing God." 1 Pet. ii, 18, 19: "Servants, be subject to your masters with all fear; not only to the good and gentle, but also to the froward. For this is thankworthy, if a man for conscience towards God endure grief, suffering wrongfully." We take them all together, because of their kindred phraseology and import. That these relate to a state of slavery, is clear from their import, or the common-sense meaning of the language used. In Eph. vi, 8, the apostle winds up his exhortation to the servants by this general remark: "Knowing that whatsoever good thing any man doeth, the same shall he receive of the Lord, whether he be bond or free." Here is a broad line of distinction drawn between the condition of the persons spoken of; the one is a bondman, the other a free man. But it is urged here again, that the term bond, as here used, implies nothing more than the obligation of hired service or apprenticeships. This interpretation, apart from its unsettling the meaning of the term, as used by the apostle in his letter to the Corinthians, which we have just noticed, and elsewhere, in his various letters to the churches, as it appears to us, falls very far short of the strength of the language used in these passages: "Servants, be subject to your masters according to the flesh, with fear and trembling;" and, "Servants, be subject to your masters with all fear." Now, the laws governing the relations of hired service or apprenticeship, do not invest the employer or master with such authority over the persons in his employ or service, as to require them to "fear and tremble, with all fear," &c., when they come into his presence; and, for this reason, is of doubtful application. But if we understand it as relating to slavery, where the laws, as they always do, so far as our reading on the subject of slavery is concerned, give the master, in some sort, a right over the life of his slave, there is some relevancy in the language used. He may well be subject "with fear and trembling," "with all fear," lest his life pay the forfeiture of any seeming inattention to, or want of respect for his master's authority.

Whatever others may think as to the merit of this criticism, to us there is some force in it; as it gives an easy and natural sense to the language employed. In something after the shape of an accidental discussion with the Rev. Edward Smith, on the sinfulness of slavery under all circumstances, so as to exclude the persons connected with it from the Church of God, he took the ground that these passages did not relate to a state of slavery. We threw this criticism in his way, and he was so pressed with the difficulty, that he could not, and did not, attempt to meet it in any other way than by roundly, repeatedly, and flatly denying, that the master here spoken of was the object of the servant's fear; contending that when Paul says, "Servants, be subject to your masters according to the flesh, with fear and trembling;" and that Peter, when he said, "Servants, be subject unto your masters with all fear; not only to the good and gentle, but also to the froward," had reference to God, and to God only, as the object of their fear. And after making one of his longest and strongest efforts to establish this garbling, by arguing that man was not to fear his fellow-man, proceeded to prove that God was the object of fear spoken of in these passages, by the following quotations: "Be not afraid of him that can kill the body, and after that hath no more that he can do; but fear him, that after he hath killed, hath power to cast into hell; yea, I say unto you, fear him;" and, "The fear of man bringeth a snare;" passages as irrelevant as the gloss was unjustifiable; and, on his part, an act of daring presumption on the ignorance and gullibility of the audience, unsurpassed in the history of such discussions. For a school-boy, ten years old, capable of understanding the ideas conveyed by plain language, could and would tell you, that in those passages the master, and not God, is the object of the servant's fear.

But furthermore, this garbling involves, necessarily, the following very gross absurdity, namely, that there are many Gods of opposite character. "Servants, be subject to your masters with all fear," that is, (according to the Rev. E. Smith,) to God; "not only to the good and gentle Gods, but also to the froward Gods; for this is thankworthy, if a man for conscience toward (some other) God endure grief, suffering wrongfully." Now this extended application of the gloss, while it appears to us to be legitimate, renders the interpretation what it is in truth, supremely ridiculous. And it may well excite our wonder, how a man of his acknowledged abilities, and large pretensions,—for he told us in the discussion, that he had more books than any Methodist preacher he ever knew—that his library would weigh over a ton; and made some remarks about his head, as being equal to his number of books, and the weight of his library; (big words from a large man, in a tall way, for intimidation and effect,)—could possibly embrace, announce, and labour long and hard to prove a doctrine, so manifestly at war with the plain common-sense understanding of the language used, and so ruinous to the essential character of the God of the Bible. The difficulty would have been fully solved to the reader had he been present, and heard the Rev. brother give the history of his becoming an abolitionist.

He had been in all thirty years a preacher of the gospel. Twenty years of that time he had been a good anti-slavery man; the last ten years an abolitionist. So that during the space of twenty years studying and preaching the gospel, with all the advantages of his number of books, the weight of his library, and the head God had given him, he could only get light enough to see that slavery was wrong, and thus become an anti-slavery man. Some abolition documents, according to his own showing, were the honoured instruments of his conversion. And so easy was his faith, and ready the disposition of his heart to receive from this source what he had failed to learn from the Bible during the space of twenty years reading and studying it, that before he had read the half of them he was converted out and out. So that, from his own account, it mattered but little whether the unread half of those documents had been a mere rehearsal of the wondrous exploits of Robinson Crusoe, or Sinbad the Sailor: he was fully brought over, and ready to face tò the music of their teachings.

This docile state of mind preparing him to embrace the system;—his new-born zeal as a recent convert;—his loss of fraternal feeling for his former brethren;—his firmness, or strong in his own way;—together "with fancy's airy flight" of large success attending the new movement, with which the "Lion of the West" would be honourably connected; all conspired to commit him fully. And he appears to be so absorbed with the importance of the subject, that we would say, he takes all for granted without examination; and seems to think, that all the world has to do on this subject, is to hear and receive the law at his mouth, and act accordingly.

The next passage to which we call attention, is found in 1 Tim. vi, 1, 2. "Let as many servants as are under the yoke, count their own masters worthy of all honour, that the name of God and his doctrine be not blasphemed. And they that have believing masters, let them not despise them, because they are brethren; but rather do them service, because they are faithful and beloved; partakers of the benefit." Here the obligation of the servant "under the yoke," (a form of expression decisive of the slavery relation,) to obey both heathen and Christian, or believing masters, is not only distinctly and clearly stated, but argued to vindicate the divinity, practical utility, and excellence of the doctrines of the gospel they were to teach, "that the name of God and his doctrine be not blasphemed." And also the Christian character of the believing master is fully endorsed, "as brethren faithful and beloved," and as having stronger claims on their fidelity,—"rather do them service,"—from this very consideration.

So that it unquestionably appears from this passage, (if the relation here spoken of be that of slavery,) that the apostolic practice was to take both believing master and servant (or slave) into the Church, as the rightful partakers of its common privileges and blessings. And that such is its import, appears to us to be so very clear and conclusive from its face, as not to admit of rational quibble or doubt; and which, in our next chapter, we will show to be the opinion and interpretation of the most learned and accredited lights of the Church and the world.

And this view of the subject derives no inconsiderable degree of strength from the language of the apostle Peter, when he speaks of "good and gentle masters," in contradistinction from "froward masters." For when we reflect on the very discriminating use made of words and phrases in the Christian revelation, it is not fairly to be presumed that the apostle used this phraseology in that loose sense which would exclusively apply to those traits of character which we sometimes witness in men, apart from the converting grace of God.

Another argument of great weight, in favour of the interpretation we have here given of the import of these various passages, is, that the obligation, or duty of servants to obey their masters, is nowhere in them urged from considerations of right, but from principles of moral goodness, etc. For the proof or correctness of this position, the reader is referred to the section containing the argument against the Divine right of slavery, as drawn from the law of revelation. Now, if this view of the subject be correct, the language of those various passages cannot well be understood as applying to hired service or apprenticeships. In these relations there is a principle of right involved. If I stipulate with a man for so much wages, for a certain amount of labour to be performed; or take an indented apprentice for a specified time, to teach him my art or profession, whatever it may be; they are responsible, on principles of right, to be faithful. Now a law enforcing their obligation to fidelity, that did not involve this principle of right, would be too loose to meet or cover the case, and therefore, in a civil sense, of no practical utility. Such we claim to be the fact in relation to the question before us; and for this reason, that those passages of Scripture in controversy do not relate to these civil relations, but to that of slavery. Mark! it is not intended to be said that they can have no application to those relations; but, for the reasons above stated, that they were not originally intended to, and do not, exclusively apply to them.

Now, from the very clear, distinct, and unequivocal manner in which this subject is presented, in the Patriarchal, Jewish, and Christian dispensations, it is somewhat difficult to conceive how a contrary opinion ever obtained, especially among men of sober and mature reflection, who, from the heart, implicitly receive the Holy Scriptures as a revelation from God. That superficial minds, which, on this subject, jump at conclusions, without the labour of examining it in its connexion with the principles of God's moral and providential government, should see some difficulties hanging about it, is to be looked for on this as well as all other subjects that do not lie on the surface, so as to be fully scanned and comprehended at one glance of their self-supposed flaming penetration. But, that men of sound judgment and patient thought should be led away by first appearances, has been to us a matter of some surprise, and which has led us to inquire after the reasons in the premises. And the result of our cogitations is, that a remark we read, in the days of our youth, in the works of Mr. Fletcher, on another subject, is true of this subject:—"That nothing is more common than for men, under the plausible pretence of avoiding an extreme, rushing into the other, or opposite extreme." Now, we fear, it has been too generally taken for granted, that if we admit that those Scriptures really do, and especially the gospel dispensation, endorse the Christian character of a master in the relation, we are thereby compelled to recognize the Divine right of slavery, as an institution specially appointed by God, as the Moral Governor of the universe.

We, however, as we shall endeavour to prove in the sequel, to the satisfaction of the attentive reader, do not think this conclusion necessarily follows.

SECTION VII.

CRITICAL AUTHORITIES.

In our last sections we briefly reviewed those passages of Scripture, found in the Old and New Testaments, which involve the slavery relation, and, as we claim, were given for its regulation; and have endeavoured, by a variety of critical and argumentative remarks, to sustain the correctness of our position; and which, to our own mind, we have made clear beyond reasonable doubt. We will next present to the reader's attention the views of several of the most distinguished and learned commentators, theologians, and lexicographers the Church and the world have produced for centuries. Indeed, had we time and space, we might collate the whole tribe of them; for we believe there is not a single author extant, of properly accredited and acknowledged critical ability in biblical and literary acquirements, who materially differs from their general views on this grave subject. Hence our recent reformers discard their authority; with what propriety, let a sober and candid public decide. And the more so, inasmuch as, if our present translation be incorrect, language has its laws of evidence, by which the true import of these several passages can be fairly tried and decided, and the question in this way satisfactorily adjusted.

We will first quote from the notes of Macknight.

Eph. vi, 5: "Servants, obey your masters," &c. As the Gospel does not cancel the civil rights of mankind, I say to bond-servants, Obey your masters, who have the property of your body, "with fear and trembling," as liable to be punished by them for disobedience.

Colos. iii, 22: "Servants, obey in all things," &c. Though the word in the original properly signifies a slave, our English translators, in all places where the duties of slaves are inculcated, have justly translated it servant; because anciently the Greeks and Romans had scarce any servants but slaves; and because the duties of the hired servant, during the time of his service, are the same as those with the slave. So that what the apostle said to the slave, was in effect said to the hired servant. Upon these principles, in translations of the Scriptures designed for countries where slavery is abolished, and servants are freemen, the word in the original may with truth be translated servant. In this and the parallel passage, Eph. vi, 5, the apostle is very particular in his precepts to slaves and lords; because in all the countries where slavery was established, many of the slaves were exceedingly addicted to fraud, lying, and stealing; and many of the masters were tyrannical and cruel to their slaves. Perhaps, also, he was thus particular in his precepts to slaves, because the Jews held perpetual slavery to be unlawful, and because the Judaizing teachers propagated that doctrine in the Church. But from the apostle's precepts it may be inferred, that if slaves are justly acquired, they may be lawfully retained; as the gospel does not make void any of the civil rights of mankind.

1 Tim. vi, 1, 2: Let whatever Christian slaves are under the yoke of unbelievers pay their own masters all respect and obedience, &c.

2. And those Christian slaves who have believing masters, let them not despise them, fancying that they

are equals because they are brethren in Christ; for though all Christians are equal as to religious privileges, slaves are inferior to their masters as to station.

Titus ii, 9: "Exhort servants to be obedient," &c. Slaves exhort to be subject to their own masters, and in all things lawful, to be careful to please them, &c.

1 Pet. ii, 18: Household slaves, be subject to your own lords with all reverence, although they be unbelievers; and give obedience not only to the humane and gentle, but also to the ill-natured and severe.

We quote next from Burkitt.

1 Tim. vi, 1: Christianity frees persons from sinful slavery or bondage, but not from civil servitude and subjection. Observe the general duty required of all servants towards their masters. 1. Their infidel or unbelieving masters; they are required to carry it dutifully and respectfully toward them. 2. Their believing and Christian masters; they should not despise them because they are brethren.

Tit. ii, 9: "Exhort servants," &c. The souls of the poorest servants, or slaves, for whom Christ died, must be of precious account with him, &c.

1 Pet. ii, 18: "Servants, be subject," &c. Thus let Christian servants be subject to their masters, whether Christian or heathen, giving due reverence and respect.

The following is from Thomas Scott's Notes and Observations:—

Lev. xxv, 44–46: The Israelites were permitted to keep slaves of other nations, perhaps in order to typify that none but the true Israel of God participate of that liberty with which Christ has made his people free. But it was also allowed, that in this manner the Gentiles might become acquainted with the true religion: and when the Israelites copied the example of their pious progenitors, there can be no reasonable doubt that it was overruled to the eternal salvation of many souls.

1 Cor. vii, 21, 22: If then any one had been converted in a state of slavery, (which was the common case of servants in those days, that is, of a very large majority, in many cities and countries,) and he was the property of a heathen master, let him be less solicitous about his liberty, than about glorifying God in that trying situation. But if he was able, or had a fair opportunity of obtaining his liberty, he would do well to embrace it. The converted slave, however, was called to the noblest liberty as a freedman of Christ, and emancipated from Satan's yoke.

Eph. vi, 5–9: The apostle next exhorts servants, who had embraced Christianity, to be obedient unto their own masters according to the flesh, that is, to whom they were subjected in temporal matters. In general, the servants at that time were slaves, the property of their masters; and were often treated with great severity, though seldom with that systematic cruelty which commonly attends slavery in these days. But the apostles were ministers of religion, not politicians; they had not that influence among legislators and rulers, which would have been requisite for the abolition of slavery. Indeed, in that state of society as to other things, this would not have been expedient; God did not please miraculously to interpose in this case; and they were not required to exasperate their persecutors, by expressly contending against the lawfulness of slavery. Yet both the law of love, and the gospel of grace, tend to its abolition as far as they are known and regarded; and the universal prevalence of Christianity must annihilate slavery, with many other evils, which in the present state of things cannot be wholly avoided.

In the wisdom of God, the apostles were left to take such matters as they found them, and to teach servants and masters their respective duties, in the performance of which the evil would be mitigated, till in due time it should be extirpated by Christian legislators. And after various instructions, as to the manner in which servants or slaves should be governed by the principles of Christianity in doing their duty, he remarks, on the other hand, believing masters ought to act from the same principles, and in the same conscientious manner toward their servants, whether these were Christians or not; exercising their authority with humanity and gentleness.

Col. iii, 22–25. Thus the poor slave who singly aimed to please God, even in obeying the unreasonable commands of a harsh and severe master.

1 Tim. vi, 1–5. The apostle next directed, that Christians who were "under the yoke" of slavery, should quietly attend to the duties of their lowly situation; counting their own masters entitled to all the respect, fidelity, and obedience, which that superior relation demanded, and not supposing their religious knowledge, privileges, or liberty, gave them a right to despise their heathen masters, to speak or act disrespectfully to them; to disobey their lawful commands, or to expose their faults to their neighbours. This they ought to attend to, that the name of God might not be blasphemed, and his truth and worship reviled among the Gentiles, by means of the failure of Christian servants in acknowledged duties. And such of

them as enjoyed the privilege of believing masters, ought by no means to despise them, or withhold from them due respect and obedience, because they were brethren in Christ, and so upon a level in respect to religious privileges; but rather to do them service with double diligence and cheerfulness, because of their faith in Christ, and their interest in his love, as partakers of the inestimable benefits of his salvation. This shows that Christian masters are not required to set their slaves at liberty; though they were instructed to behave toward them in such a manner as would greatly lessen and nearly annihilate the evils of slavery. It would have excited much confusion, awakened the jealousy of the civil powers, and greatly retarded the progress of Christianity, had the liberation of slaves by the converts been expressly required by the apostles; though the principles of the law and the gospel, when carried to their consequences, will infallibly abolish slavery. These things Timothy was directed to teach and enforce, as matters of the greatest importance; and if any persons taught otherwise, and consented not to such salutary words, which were indeed the words of Christ speaking by him, and an essential part of the doctrine according to godliness, he must be considered as a self-conceited, ignorant man, who, being puffed up with an opinion of his own abilities, was ambitious of distinction and applause, though entirely unacquainted with the real nature and tendency of the gospel. The picture here drawn of the great body of the croakers, so far as we have heard them on this subject, is to the life; the likeness is perfect.

1 Peter ii, 18–25. The apostle Peter exhorted servants to obedience, even in stronger language than his beloved brother Paul had done. These were general-

ly slaves, and many of them to heathen masters, who used them very cruelly.

Next we quote from the Comprehensive Commentaries.

1 Tim. vi, 1, 2: "Let as many servants," &c. If Christianity finds servants under the yoke, it continues them under it; for the gospel does not cancel the obligations any be under, either by the law of nature or mutual consent. If servants that embraced the Christian religion should grow insolent or disobedient to their masters, the doctrine of Christ would be reflected on for their sakes, as it had made men worse livers than they had been before they received the gospel. Or suppose the master was a believer and the servant a believer too; would not that excuse him; because in Christ there is neither bond nor free? No, by no means: they that have believing masters let them not despise them, because they are brethren; for that brotherhood relates only to spiritual privileges, not to any outward dignity or advantage; nay, rather do them service because they are faithful and beloved. They must think themselves the more obliged to serve them, because the faith and love that bespeak men Christians, oblige them to do good, and that is all wherein their service consists.

We will now introduce to the attention of the reader the views of Dr. Adam Clarke on this subject.

Gen. xvii, 13. "He that is bought with money"—a slave.

Isaiah lviii, 6: "Is not this the fast that I have chosen? to loose the bands of wickedness, to undo the heavy burdens, and to let the oppressed go free, and that ye break every yoke?" The Dr. commences his notes on this chapter, "Cry aloud, spare not. Never was there a louder cry against the hypocrisy, nor a more cutting reproof of the wickedness of a people, professing a national established religion, having all the forms of godliness without a particle of its power." And then on the sixth verse he says: "How can any nation pretend to fast, or worship God at all, or dare to profess that they believe in the existence of such a being, while they carry on what is called the slave-trade, and traffic in the souls, blood, and bodies of men? O, ye most flagitious of knaves, and worst of hypocrites; cast off at once the mask of religion, and deepen not your endless perdition by professing the faith of our Lord Jesus Christ, while ye continue in this traffic."

1 Cor. vii, 21: "Art thou called being a servant? care not for it; but if thou mayest be made free, use it rather." Art thou converted to Christ while thou art a slave; the property of another person, and bought with his money? care not for it. This will not injure thy Christian condition; but if thou canst obtain thy liberty, use it rather: prefer this state for the sake of freedom, and the temporal advantages connected with it.

Verse 22: "For he that is called"—the man who, being a slave, is converted to the Christian faith,—"is the Lord's free man;" his condition as a slave does not vitiate any of the privileges to which he is entitled as a Christian. On the other hand, all free men who receive the grace of Christ, must consider themselves the slaves of the Lord, *i. e.* his real property, to be employed and disposed of according to his godly wisdom.

In these verses the apostle shows that the Christian religion does not abolish our civil connexions; in reference to them, where it finds us there it leaves us. In whatever relation we stand before our embracing Christianity, there we stand still: our secular condition being no further changed than as it may be effected by the melioration of our moral character, &c. As the reader can see by reference to his commentaries.

In his general remarks at the close of the chapter, we find the following paragraphs :—

"The conversion which the Scriptures require, though it makes a most essential change in our souls, in reference to God, and in our works, in reference both to God and man, makes none in our civil state: even if a man is called, i. e. converted in a state of slavery, he does not gain his manumission in consequence of his conversion; he stands in the same relation, both to the state and his fellows, that he stood in before; and is not to assume any civil rights or privileges, in consequence of the conversion of his soul to God. The apostle decides the matter in this chapter, and orders that every man should abide in the same calling wherein he is called."

"I have entered the more fully into this subject, because it, or allusions to it, are frequently occurring in the New Testament. And I speak it here once for all. And to conclude, I here register my testimony against the unprincipled, inhuman, anti-christian, and diabolical slave-trade, with all its authors, promoters, abettors, and sacrilegious gains, as well as against the great devil, the father of it and them."

Eph. vi, 5–8: "Servants, be obedient," &c. Though the original frequently signifies a slave or bondman, yet it often implies a servant in general, or any one bound to another, either for a limited time or for life. Even a slave, if a Christian, was bound to serve him faithfully; by whose money he was bought, howsoever illegal that traffic may be considered. In heathen countries slavery is, in some sort, excusable; among Christians it is an enormity and a crime, for which perdition has scarcely an adequate place of punishment.

"With fear and trembling," because the law gives them the power to punish you for every act of disobedience.

Verse 8. Whether he be bond,—a slave bought with money.

Colossians iv, 1: "Masters, give unto your servants that which is just and equal," &c. As it is bondmen or slaves of whom the apostle speaks, we may at once see with what propriety this exhortation is given. The condition of slaves among the Greeks and Romans was wretched in the extreme. They could appeal to no law, and they could neither expect justice nor equity.

1 Tim. vi, 1, 2. The word (in the original) here means, slaves converted to the Christian faith; and the yoke is that state of slavery; and by masters, despots, we are to understand the heathen masters of those Christianized slaves. Even these, in such circumstances, and under such domination, are commanded to treat their masters with all honour and respect; that the name of God, by which they were called, and the doctrine of God, Christianity, which they had professed, might not be blasphemed; might not be evilly spoken of in consequence of their misconduct. Civil rights are never abolished by any communications from the Spirit of God. The civil state in which a man was before his conversion, is not altered by that conversion, nor does the grace of God absolve him

from any claims which either the state or his neighbour had upon him. All these outward things continue unaltered.

Verse 2. "And they that have believing masters, [who have been lately converted, as well as themselves,] let them not despise them," supposing themselves to be their equals, because they are their brethren in Christ, and grounding their opinion on this, that in him there is neither male nor female, bond nor free; but although all are equal as to their spiritual privileges and state, yet there still continues, in the order of God's providence, a great disparity in their station; for the master must ever be, in this sense, superior to the servants. But rather do them service—obey them the more cheerfully, because they are faithful and beloved; faithful to God's grace—beloved by him and his true followers.

Titus ii, 9: "Exhort servants to be obedient." The apostle refers to those who were slaves, and the property of their masters; even these are exhorted to be faithful to their own despots, though they had no right over them on the grounds of natural justice.

We have been thus particular in quoting thus largely from the notes of Dr. Clarke, for the following reasons:

First. He is often quoted by the True Wesleyans, and others who sympathize with them in their peculiar views, as supporting their position.

Secondly. He is proclaimed as being contradictory, or inconsistent with himself, in his views on the subject of slavery; in all of which they, as we think, are guilty of either ignorantly or wickedly misrepresenting him, as we shall proceed to prove.

A careful, candid, and impartial examination of his

notes and observations on this subject will give us the following analysis :

1. That the slave-trade, or incipient movements in this inhuman and diabolic traffic, is a crime of the greatest magnitude; against which he enters his solemn protest.

2. That although in heathen countries—that is, in heathen governments—slavery is in some sort excusable ; it is in Christian countries—that is, when established by Christian governments—an enormity and crime, for which perdition has scarcely an adequate place of punishment.

3. But when it exists as an element of organized society—however reprehensible the Christian country or government, which has established the relation, may in their public capacity be,—an individual who is connected with it, by the operation of public law, may be a good Christian, faithful to the grace of God, and, as such, entitled to all the privileges of the Christian Church.

Now it is confidently believed that, in substance, this analysis comprehends all he has ever written, in his commentaries or elsewhere, on this subject. And with what pretensions he can be represented as favouring the True Wesleyan or kindred movements, we are at an utter loss to conceive. As we think, no man understanding what he has written can honestly believe it ; much less, without violating the commandment, " Thou shalt not bear false witness against thy neighbour," so represent him to the world.

And as to the charge of contradiction and inconsistency, it is equally a gratuitous misrepresentation. For, as we have seen, his position is, that the first acts of aggression, or the slave-trade, is essential wickedness; that a state of slavery is contrary to natural justice; therefore Christian countries or governments, which establish or continue such a relation, are guilty of a great enormity. But when it has once obtained as an element of civil society, and is providentially in the hands of those who did not create or cannot control this state of things, or, in other words, in the hands of a portion of the people, it may exist aside from its abuses, without prejudice to the Christian character of those in the relation.

We will next quote from Mr. Benson.

1 Cor. vii, 21–44: "Art thou called being a servant? [or bond-man, as the word properly signifies,] care not for it; [do not much regard it, nor anxiously seek liberty: do not suppose that such a condition renders thee less acceptable to God, or is unworthy of a Christian;] but if thou mayest be made free, [by any lawful method,] use it rather. [Embrace the opportunity.] He that is called in [or by] the Lord, to Christian saving faith, being a servant or bondman, is the Lord's freeman, being delivered by him from the slavery of sin and Satan, and therefore possesses the greatest of all dignities. Likewise—in like manner,—he that is called, being free from the authority of any human master, is Christ's servant or bondman; not free in this respect; not at his own disposal; not at liberty to do his own will, but bound to be obedient and subject to Christ. Surely, as Goodwin observes, 'the apostle could not have expressed in stronger terms his deep conviction of the small importance of human distinctions than he here does: when speaking of what seems, to great and generous minds, the most miserable lot, even that of a slave, he says, Care not for it.' To which Doddridge adds, 'If liberty itself, the first of all temporal blessings,

be not of so great importance, as that a man, blessed with the high hopes and glorious consolations of Christianity, should make himself very solicitous about it, how much less upon those comparatively trifling distinctions on which many lay so disproportionate, so extravagant a stress.'"

"Brethren, let every man," &c. Here the apostle repeats the same advice a third time in the compass of a few verses, intending, L'Enfant thinks, to correct some disorders among the Christian slaves at Corinth, who, agreeably to the doctrine of the false teachers, claimed their liberty, on pretence that as brethren in Christ they were on an equality with their Christian masters.

Eph. vi, 5–8: "Servants," &c. Bond-servants, or he may include also those who were in the station of hired servants; be obedient to your masters; for the gospel does not cancel the civil rights of man, whether he be bond or free, a slave or freeman; whether he be the greatest prince or the meanest servant.

1 Tim. vi, 1, 2: Because the law of Moses did not allow Israelites to be made slaves for life without their own consent, it seems the Judaizing teachers, with a view to allure slaves to their party, encouraged them in disobeying the commands of their masters. This doctrine the apostle condemns here, as in his other Epistles, by enjoining Christian slaves to obey their masters, whether believers or unbelievers. Let servants, or slaves rather, under the yoke of heathen masters, count them worthy of all honour,—all the honour due from a servant to a master—that the name of God and his doctrine be not blasphemed, that is, evil spoken of, as tending to destroy the political rights

of mankind. And they that have believing masters—which for any to have is a great privilege—let them not despise them—pay them the less obedience—because they are brethren in Christ, believers, and in that respect on a level with them. They that live in a religious community know the danger of this, and that greater grace is requisite to bear with the faults of a brother, than a man of the world or even an infidel.

We will next quote from Richard Watson. In his "Biblical and Theological Dictionary," on the word servant, he remarks:—

"This word generally signifies a slave. For formerly, among the Hebrews and neighbouring nations, the greater part of servants were slaves; that is to say, they belonged absolutely to their masters, who had a right to dispose of their persons, their bodies, goods, and even of their lives, in some cases."

From his Life, or one of his addresses as contained in his Life, by Jackson, he says, "Our opinions as a body [the Wesleyan Connexion in England] respecting slavery as a system, have long been known throughout the West Indies. But as it is equally known, by all persons who will do us justice, that our missionaries are restrained from agitating all abstract questions of this kind, both in public and private; and that we hold it as a most sacred Christian duty, that obedience should be paid by slaves to their owners, and that seditions and insurrections are crimes of the highest nature, no exceptions have ever been taken to our missionaries on this account."—Page 296.

Again, on the same and following page:—

"Wherever policy may be proper, we think it out of place in the proceedings of a religious body; and wish it most clearly to be understood, that while we ask protection for our missions, on the ground of their inculcating peace and good order in the colonies, and our missionaries being restrained from all interference with the civil concerns of the population, our society in this country is but of one sentiment on the subject of slavery as a system."

Servant. In Scripture a slave—a bondman.—*Webster.*

In this collection of names, renowned as men of superior literary and critical attainments, we have omitted the name of Wesley, for the reason that his tract on slavery would not properly range under the head of critical authorities. It, as a whole, speaks for itself, with regard to the abandoned iniquity of the system, in its beginning and end. And we could wish that his tract was written on the heart of every slaveholder, their aiders and abettors. Doubtless it would soon put an end to the accursed system. That tract, however, is particularly addressed to the first movements, or incipient measures of the system.

As before intimated, we might have greatly swelled the number of our critical authorities. But these we think sufficient. And the special object we had in view, was not to endorse their respective and peculiar views of slavery, but the true import and application of the term servant, as found in the various passages of Scripture we have quoted in this investigation; together with the Christian character of those in the relation, and the apostolic practice of receiving them into the Church. And, as the reader will have seen, they each and all sustain the position we have taken on that subject.

It being probably the most appropriate department,

we will, in this connexion, devote a few moments' attention to the historical aspects of this question. In the march of its agitation, the voice of history has been appealed to, for the weight of its authority in its adjudication, and is claimed, with his usual confidence, by the Rev. Edward Smith, as supporting the ultra-abolition measures. For he tells us, in his published address, entitled, "The Bible against Slavery," delivered in the Sixth Presbyterian Church of Cincinnati, March 19, 1843, "I have examined no less than twenty thousand pages of octavos and quartos, to ascertain one single fact,—to know whether Grecian or Roman slavery extended to, and existed in the provinces of the Roman Empire, in which the churches were located to which these regulations were given. Six of Paul's Epistles were written to churches in Europe; namely, one to Rome, two to Corinth, two to Thessalonica, and one to Philippi .... We will now cross the Hellespont, and go into Asia Minor. Here the churches were located to which these regulations were given: the Epistles in which the regulations under consideration are found, were all addressed to churches located in Asia Minor. But in these countries neither Roman nor Grecian slavery existed. These were the last countries conquered by the Roman arms. Here Augustus Cæsar robed himself in the imperial purple, and made these countries Roman provinces twenty-eight years before the birth of Christ; and from that time slavery began to decline. It was the policy of the Roman Empire to allow the conquered provinces to retain, for the most part, their own religion and laws, under Roman masters. It was emphatically an empire of religious toleration." (This is far from being true, as the persecutions that obtained under different emperors, both at home and abroad, abundantly prove.) "The ancient laws of these countries prohibited slavery, as well as in the kingdom of Egypt; and when conquered by the Greeks and Romans, slavery was not introduced into them; so that at the time of writing these Epistles they were free from slavery. They were free provinces of the Roman Empire. And if slavery was not in the country, it could not get into the Church. Those who say that St. Paul took slaveholders into the Church, take the affirmative of this question, and must prove that slavery existed in these provinces. This they cannot do. I challenge them to the task. And though I am not bound to prove a negative, I could prove, had I access to my own library, that there was none there. I say, my own library, because I have the proofs marked, and could turn to them with but little trouble."

We desire to examine this very singular extract in various points of light, besides the one above pointed out in reference to religious toleration.

First: As to the palpable contradictions contained in it. He tells us,—1. In these countries neither Roman nor Grecian slavery existed. 2. The ancient laws of these countries prohibited slavery; and when conquered by the Greeks and Romans, slavery was not introduced into them; and yet, twenty-eight years before Christ, when Augustus Cæsar made them Roman provinces, "from that time slavery began to decline." Query: If it was prohibited by their ancient laws; if neither Roman nor Grecian slavery existed there; and if, when these countries were conquered by the Greeks and Romans, it was not introduced into them, how did it get there? And if it was not there, how could it "begin to decline?" A solution of these queries, by so profound an historian as the Rev. brother, would doubtless throw some light on this question; unless, in self-contradiction, it should claim too near a relationship to the above. In that event, the darkness would be doubly profound.

Second: He tells us he is not bound to prove a negative. We are not satisfied that he is correct in this declaration. It may be true that, as a mere debater, or partisan, he was not bound to do so. But we have yet to learn, that it is compatible with the character of a reformer or Christian minister, on any question of morals or religion, to resort to such trickery or manœuvring, to sustain himself or his position. Our reflections have led us to an entirely different conclusion; one in which we think we shall be supported by the intelligence of the world; namely, that, as a reformer or minister, if he actually is in possession of the proofs above claimed,—proofs that must have considerable weight on this great moral question, it is his imperative duty, by satisfactory references to the authorities which he has in his "own library, marked," and to which he can turn "with little trouble," to furnish them for the benefit of the race. And that he cannot be innocent in withholding this intelligence, and the good its communication to the world would do, is proved by the language of the apostle James: "To him that knoweth to do good and doeth it not, to him it is sin."

It being now about the sixth year since his address was published, and the fact, according to his own statement, of his having the proofs marked, so as to be able to turn to them with little trouble, is proof that he cannot plead want of time as a reason why he has not performed this good service to the world before this day. And if, as he claims, he has those proofs marked, we are very confident, that so far as the time is concerned that would be required to give those proofs to the world, his labour in so doing would be of a hundred-fold more importance to mankind than anything else claiming his attention for the same length of time.

And he cannot plead, as an excuse in this matter, that it had slipped his memory. For in the discussion before alluded to, when this matter was introduced, we objected to the repetition of this stale assertion, alleging that he had had time enough (between five and six years) to furnish the world with his proofs, by giving the name of the authors, with the chapter and verse. His reply was, that he could not bring a cart-load of books to settle the question. Our rejoinder was, that the fact then admitted by the Rev. brother, that it was scattered through a cart-load of books, was proof positive that he had not the plain, straightforward, outstanding voice of history, as he claimed. And we will here record it as our sober conviction, that unless the Rev. brother does furnish us with the proofs which, in his own library, he has so readily at command, his big words on this subject were merely tricks of oratory; and that in entertaining this opinion, we shall be sustained by the intelligence of the world.

Another remark which we would here make is, that the brother and Rollin do not agree as to dates. He tells us that Augustus Cæsar made these countries of Asia Minor Roman provinces twenty-eight years before Christ. Rollin tells us that Cappadocia, which was one of the provinces of Asia Minor, was reduced into a Roman province sixteen years before Christ. Book xxi, art. iii, vol. vii, p. 331.

We will, in the next place, see if his statements relative to the non-existence of slavery in the provinces of Asia Minor, in which those churches were located to which the Epistles containing those directions on the subject of slavery were addressed, are sustained by the voice of history. And we may feel ourselves at the greater liberty in this, from his published challenge to the world.

Not being much of an historian, and having, from our location, but little access to works of this kind, we shall not attempt a thorough historical examination of the question.

It will be borne in mind by the intelligent reader, that, in the above extract, it is said, "The ancient laws of these countries prohibited slavery; and when conquered by the Greeks and Romans, slavery was not introduced into them. So that at the time of writing these Epistles they were free from slavery." And again: "But in these countries neither Grecian nor Roman slavery existed." Now, according to Rollin, eighty-eight years before Christ, slavery must have been very extensive in these provinces; for, in his twenty-third book, vol. ii, p. 313, when writing the history of Pontus, which was one of these provinces, we have the following language:—

"Mithridates, considering that the Romans and Italians in general, who were at that time in Asia Minor upon different affairs, carried on secret intrigues, much to the prejudice of his interests, sent private orders from EPHESUS, where he then was, to the governors of the provinces, and magistrates of the cities of Asia Minor, to massacre them all upon a fixed day. The women, children, and *domestics* were included in this proscription. To these orders was annexed a prohibition not to give interment to those who should be killed. Their estates and effects were to be confiscated for the use of the king and the murderers. A severe fine was levied upon such as should conceal the living, or bury the dead; and a reward appointed for whoever discovered those who were hid. *Liberty was given to the slaves who killed their masters;* and debtors forgiven half their debts for killing their creditors. The repetition only of this dreadful order is enough to make one shudder with horror. What then must have been the desolation in all those provinces where it was put in execution! Fourscore thousand Romans and Italians were butchered in consequence of it. Some make the slain amount to almost twice that number."

Now it is very clear from this quotation, whether the ancient laws of these countries prohibited slavery or not, that, in the cities and provinces of Asia Minor, slaves were very numerous eighty-eight years before Christ. And he further tells us, in the same book, that in the year 72 B. C., some sixteen years later, they were so plenty, as to sell only for four drachmas, that is, about twenty-eight pence sterling per slave.—Vol. ii, p. 321. How they got there, when they got there, and by what authority it existed, are questions on which he gives us no distinct information. It is clear, however, from these quotations, that it existed very extensively in connexion with the Roman and Italian population, which must have been very numerous, for the offer of liberty to be tendered to all slaves who would join in this plot of death against their masters.

And the fact that their liberty was offered as an incentive to, and as the reward of this massacre, is strong presumptive evidence that slavery existed there by law. And another argument of some weight in support of this presumption is, that the Romans and Italians would hardly have taken so great an amount of slaves with them to a distant country, where slavery was prohibited by law. And if, as appears possible from the quotations, those Romans and Italians, on emigrating, took slaves with them to that country when under foreign jurisdiction, what is the legitimate inference touching their practice in this matter, after those provinces were conquered, and became subject to Roman jurisdiction? So that the facts and probabilities that bear upon this question are at war with Brother Smith's statements; indeed, his statements, as before shown, are at war with themselves; and taken in connexion with these quotations from Rollin, they constitute a perfect jumble of contradictions.

Another authority we would introduce, is from Neander's Church History, translated by Rose, p. 66.

"In Smyrna the proconsul seems to have been too sensible to lend his ear to such reports. A young man of some rank, by name Bettius Pegatus, although not arrested as a Christian, felt himself bound, on hearing of these accusations, to come forward in attestation of the innocence of his brethren. He asked a hearing, in which he promised to show that nothing criminal took place at the meetings of the Christians; but the legate, without giving him a hearing, only asked if he were a Christian, and on his clear declaration of this, he was cast into prison as the advocate of Christians. Some heathen slaves, under fear of the torture, declared their *Christian masters* guilty of crimes which vague rumour laid to their charge. Little as such a declaration was worth, fanaticism was eager to receive it as an evidence of truth, and the people felt that every cruelty was now justifiable,—neither kindred, age, nor sex was spared."

This is recorded as having taken place A. D. 177; and the Smyrna in question, we believe, was in Asia Minor; and if so, there appear to have been slaves there at the date above mentioned, who were owned by *Christian* masters. So that, if the Rev. brother's historical statements were consistent with themselves, and, as such, of a character to merit attention, the counter testimony of the authors quoted, in connexion with the writings of Paul and Peter, would render their reliability extremely doubtful, not to say entirely unworthy of credit.

PART SECOND.

ARGUMENTS AGAINST THE DIVINE RIGHT OF SLAVERY, AS AN INSTITUTION OF GOD, OR OF SPECIAL DIVINE APPOINTMENT.

SECTION I.

FIRST ARGUMENT, DRAWN FROM THE LAW OF NATURE.

Though we cannot now quote authorities, our reading and hearsay have led us to the opinion that there are some who believe in the Divine right of slavery; that it is of special Divine appointment, or an institution of God;* and, as such, that it is the privilege of all who can, to own and hold slaves, without prejudice to the creditability of their Christian profession. Further, we believe it has been claimed by some of the Southern ministers, (on the grounds of expediency, we suppose,) that to own slaves is an important auxiliary, if not an essential qualification, in the ministerial character, in order to the efficient and successful prosecution of its sacred duties in the slave-holding States.† While, on

* In its moral aspect, slavery was not only countenanced, permitted, and regulated by the Bible, but it was positively instituted by God himself. He had, in so many words, enjoined it.—Rev. Mr. Crowder, of Va., General Conference, 1840.

† I have become a slave-holder—a slave-holder from principle—to obviate suspicion, and gain free access to the slave, so as to do him good. It is highly advantageous to a minister that he himself should hold slaves. And I can see no impropriety, but advantage, in members, preachers, presiding elders, and even bishops, being slave-holders.—Dr. Winans, General Con. Doc., Cincinnati, 1836. James G. Birney.

Other quotations of similar sentiment might be collated, but these are sufficient.

the other hand, there are those who think that the relation of slavery, especially on the part of the master, is, under any circumstances, incompatible with a creditable profession of religion, and a visible connexion with the Christian Church; and that the Holy Scriptures, when properly understood, nowhere afford the least countenance to such a conclusion; that the thought is too shocking, too monstrous to be entertained for a moment; amounting to an impeachment of the whole character and government of God; who, rather than admit the most remote possibility of such a conclusion, contemptuously ask for a better Bible, a better Christ, a better set of prophets and apostles; in a word, a new religion, more consonant with their views of the Divine character and government.

That principles so essentially opposite cannot be found in the Christian Scriptures, when properly understood, will be admitted by all who believe in their Divine inspiration. For if truth is one, and consistent with itself, it cannot be that a book professing to teach the truth, the whole truth, and nothing but the truth, can occupy the extremes of this question as above stated. One or the other of these doctrines must be true, or both alike erroneous, or partly true and partly error, the truth lying between these extremes. Such is the conclusion to which our reading and reflection has conducted us; and the reasons which have shut us up to this faith will be seen by the attentive reader, in the preceding, as well as the following pages, which, we think, are drawn from, and sustained by, both Scripture and reason.

Being an undoctored doctor, we are aware of the delicacy of our position in differing from doctrines on this subject, venerable for their antiquity and the reputation of their authors, promulgators, and defenders. Nevertheless, we shall try, in the independent consciousness of truth, humbly to express our opinion.

Slavery, to be of Divine right, appointment, or an institution of God, should,

1. Be indicated by the laws of nature, and founded in such reasons of fitness and right as would manifest its practical utility, as best for all concerned, and vindicate the character of the Creator from the charge of partiality in his dealings with his rational creatures; or,

2. It should be plainly revealed in the Scriptures; standing out with such prominence on the page of inspiration, as to mark its intrinsic excellence as an essential part and parcel of the positive duties of society, necessary to the perfection of the Divine government, and in agreement with its settled principles, as found in the oracles of God.

Now as to its being indicated by the laws of nature, &c. This, so far as our reading is concerned, has never been seriously intimated, except by some real or pretended skeptics, who have denied to the African race the claims of humanity, or a common origin with the rest of mankind, urging their mental imbecility, as compared with those of lighter shade, or whiter skin, as evidence of their being an inferior and distinct species;—a conclusion at war with the facts in the case, and proved, beyond all controversy, to be erroneous, by living witnesses in men of colour, now on the stage, who, under all the disadvantages and discouragements peculiar to their condition, have, by dint of untiring industry, attained to a knowledge of science and letters that will compare favourably with the majority of their white brethren of better opportunities, but less application.

Another thought in this connexion, which is in refutation of the doctrine of their natural inferiority, is, that under like circumstances, they are in all respects creatures of like passions with the white race; which fact, in itself, is conclusive of a common origin.

To the Christian, if further proof be necessary, this question is settled by the voice of inspiration, which declares that God made of one blood all nations of men to dwell on all the face of the earth. Acts xvii, 26.

In addition to the above exception, it now occurs to us that a new doctrine has been advanced in the nineteenth century, by a grave Senator of South Carolina, involving the equality and natural rights of mankind, in his speech, delivered in the Senate of the United States on the Compromise bill, providing for the organization of a Territorial Government over California and New-Mexico. In that speech, where he comments on the following ever-memorable clause, found in the Declaration of American Independence,—"We hold these truths to be self-evident, that all men are created equal; that they are endowed by their Creator with certain inalienable rights; that among these are life, liberty, and the pursuit of happiness,"—he attempts to show that the above quotation is not true; that the framers of that instrument, in the use of that language, gave utterance to error on the doctrine of man's natural rights. And the pith of the argument by which he would prove them in error, and overturn the doctrines of that inimitable and venerable record, is, that all men are not created,—that they are born; some males, and some females, and in time grow up to be men and women. A quibble unworthy the man, the place, the occasion, the country, and the age. For is it not clear, that, as their descendants, we are partakers of a common nature; and, by the laws of that nature, entitled to the same rights? and moreover, that every child born into the world is virtually an act of creation; it requiring the same all-powerful energy to carry out the laws of nature, which first called them into existence?

But we cannot persuade ourselves that it was intended for anything more than a quibble. If we could, it would detract more from the senator's long-earned reputation, as a man of thought and strong mental powers, than all the other acts of his eventful life put together. True, all the circumstances considered would seem to call upon us to regard it as a frank avowal of his sentiments. But, we repeat, we cannot admit his seriousness on any other consideration but the adage, "once a man, twice a child;" the honourable senator may be an old baby—in his dotage.

Air-built or visionary as the quibble (for it deserves no higher name) of the grave senator is, it may nevertheless require a passing notice, lest the confusion of thought to which it tends may puzzle and mislead the credulous and unwary. For it is a well-known truth, that the opinions or sentiments of men of eminence and reputation for wisdom, have great influence over their admirers and common readers. Now it must be borne in mind, that the clause to which the senator's strictures and exceptions apply, is found in the Declaration of American Independence; which Declaration is intended to set forth, in an appeal to the world and the God who made it, the wrongs suffered by the American people from the Crown of Great Britain; and these wrongs as reasons why they should, and ought to, be free from the parent government; that, in the infliction of these wrongs, the government had failed of the objects for which all governments are instituted, and thereby not only justified, but—a conclusion most rational—rendered it the imperious duty of freemen to throw off the yoke of oppression, and thus dissolve their political relations. For if the powers of government are inherent in, and derived from the people, whenever that power, wheresoever lodged, ceases to seek the good of the people, it is perverted from its natural and legitimate object, and is not, and ought not to be, of longer binding force. It will therefore be seen, that the clause under consideration has reference to rights, independent of government. For, at the time they were written, there was virtually none in existence. They had rejected, or thrown off the government of England, as oppressive beyond endurance, and had not as yet organized one in its stead. It therefore, in its own language, speaks of natural rights; such as belong to us by virtue of our creation, prior to, and independent of all government.

Now the confusion of thought to which it is supposed the senator's argument, in its application to slavery, which is a creature of municipal law, may lead, is, that their natural rights may be so confounded with, or swallowed up in their civil condition, as to confuse and involve the question in such bewilderment and darkness, that ordinary readers may be lost in the gloom, or conducted to improper conclusions. Whereas, if on the one hand we look steadily at the doctrine of our natural rights, untrammelled by the interference and operation of civil government; and, on the other, at the deprivation of those rights which the African race have suffered in our country, solely by the operation of municipal law, the points will be distinct and clear, the confusion of thought above alluded to avoided, and the doctrine of our equality and natural rights not materially affected by the honourable senator's puerilities.

How, or where, to commence our search after light to illuminate our darkness on the natural right of slavery, is beyond our comprehension. After our utmost stretch of thought, not a glimmering ray breaks on our mental vision—chaotic darkness reigns entire and profound, and we are left to the conclusion that either our opacity is impenetrable, or there is not, on this subject, one scintillation of light in all the world of mind, which probably is the right conclusion. For, on reflection, it is said "We hold these truths (natural rights) to be self-evident,"—so clear and luminous in themselves, as to be incapable of additional light—so obviously and manifestly the truth, that human thought or language cannot make them more clear, intelligible, or forcible. To undertake their proof, is to "darken counsel by words without knowledge," like the skeptical philosopher's argument to prove his own existence. Said he, "I think, therefore I am," or "I exist." Here the fact that "I am," or "I exist," is a simple (or single) idea or conception; the other, "I think," therefore "I am," or "I exist," is a complex or compound one, and obscures and embarrasses the question, just in proportion to its complexity.

Hence, as the laws of nature, as we have just seen, afford no light or evidence of the natural right of slavery, but the contrary, we therefore conclude, that so far as these rights, as the gift of our Creator, are directly and primarily concerned, slavery is out of the question, being repugnant to reason and natural law. Pressed with these difficulties, the advocates of slavery have attempted its defence on other grounds, subsequent in point of time, but accidental to, and inherent in our nature;—such as might gives right, and the right a man has to dispose of himself, &c. Consequently, in the Justinian code, three origins of the right of slavery are assigned, all of which, says Sir William Blackstone, are built upon false foundations; which, we think, will so appear to the honest inquirer after truth, in the following quotation from his commentaries, in which these several rights are clearly and distinctly stated, and powerfully refuted by his able pen. And first, "slavery is held to arise from a state of captivity in war." The conqueror, say the civilians, had a right to the life of the captive; and having spared that, has a right to deal with him as he pleases. But it is an untrue position, when taken generally, that by the laws of nature or nations, a man may kill his enemy; he has only a right to kill him in particular cases; in cases of absolute necessity for self-defence; and it is plain this absolute necessity did not subsist, since the victor did not actually kill him, but made him his prisoner. War is itself justifiable only on principles of self-preservation; and therefore it gives no other right over prisoners, but merely to disable them from doing harm to us, by confining their persons; much less can it give a right to kill, torture, abuse, plunder, or even to enslave an enemy, when the war is over. Since, therefore, the right of making slaves by captivity depends upon a supposed right of slaughter, that foundation failing, the consequence drawn from it must fail likewise. But, secondly, it is said that slavery may begin by one man selling himself to another. This, if only meant of contracts to serve, or work for another, is very just; but when applied to strict slavery, in the sense of the laws of old

Rome, or modern Barbary, and we will add some of the American States, is also impossible. Every sale implies a price, an equivalent given to the seller, in lieu of what he transfers to the buyer; but what equivalent can be given for life and liberty, both of which, in absolute slavery, are held to be in the master's disposal? His property also, the very price he seems to receive, devolves to his master the instant he becomes his slave. In this case, therefore, the buyer gives nothing, and the seller receives nothing; of what validity then can a sale be, which destroys the very principle upon which all sales are founded. Lastly, besides these two ways by which slaves are acquired, they may also be hereditary: the children of acquired slaves are, by a negative kind of birthright, slaves also. But this, being built on the two former rights, must fail together with them. If neither captivity, nor the sale of one's self, can, by the laws of nature and reason, reduce the parent to slavery, much less can they reduce the offspring.

Now, if the preceding reflections and reasonings be correct, the doctrine of the rightfulness of slavery receives no countenance from the law of nature. And we are equally at a loss, when governed by the law of nature, or, in other words, recurring to first principles, to discover those reasons of fitness and right, which are indispensable to the support of its pretensions, and to mark the united wisdom and goodness of the arrangement, as equal in its operations, and the best for all concerned. We might here again propound the inquiry, to what part of the compass shall we look for light? Who is to be the slave, and for what reason? Is there anything so befitting in the relation, as to commend it to our superior judgment, and thus introduce it? Who can give an affirmative answer to these interrogatories, accompanied with such evidence as shall establish their truth beyond all controversy, and stamp them unequivocally with the seal of divinity; preserving, at the same time, the character of the Creator from the charge of partiality? To us the whole question is totally inexplicable—involved in impenetrable darkness.

Some minds, however, anxious for a plea to justify a practice so consonant with the prejudice of education, and their selfish desires on account of the supposed advantages of slavery, may attempt to resolve it into the Divine Sovereignty. But when properly understood, we think this refuge must fail also. That God is a good and a great sovereign, is not denied. Nor yet his right, as such, to tolerate such a state of things, from good and sufficient considerations, as measures of moral discipline.

Such, we think, is the teaching of the Scriptures. But we are not now examining it in the light of revelation, (of which in the sequel,) but by the laws of nature; and where, from this quarter, have we one ray of light, one word of proof, that slavery is according to the good pleasure of His sovereign will? Echo answers, Where?

SECTION II.

ARGUMENT FROM THE LAW OF REVELATION.—THE RELATION A TEMPORARY REGULATION.

HAVING, as we think, shown in the preceding observations that the Divine right—appointment—or rightfulness of slavery, is not to be found in the law of nature, we will, as indicated in the last section, now examine and see if the teaching of the Holy Scriptures warrant such a conclusion. It will be remembered that in the preceding pages we have admitted that they recognize the relation, and inculcate the duties naturally arising therefrom. But the question arises here, Is the subject so presented in the oracles of God as to justify, beyond reasonable doubt, the inference that it is of special Divine appointment, and, as such, to take rank among the positive duties of society?

This query, at first sight, may be regarded as more curious than useful; tending to perplexity and embarrassment, rather than as affording light to aid us in the elicitation and ascertainment of truth.

We, however, entertain a different opinion, believing it to lie deep at the foundation of this controversy, and of infinite importance to its thorough investigation. For if as we conceive, and have intimated, it is the a, b, c, of the whole question; or, in other words, the true point at which to commence our inquiries; inasmuch as a fair start is of singular advantage, and essential to success in any enterprise, we must in this, as in all other matters of inquiry, be saved from confusion and darkness, and arrive at more satisfactory conclusions, by commencing at the beginning.

Therefore, at this stage of our investigation, it may be useful to inquire, Are the Holy Scriptures, so far as is discoverable by the light, or indicated by the law of nature, a republication of the social duties of man? or do they intrinsically, absolutely, and permanently change those duties, so as to make that right—in all cases and under all circumstances, in our social relations—which the first constitution of things, or the law of nature, condemned as wrong? Or, in other words, was slavery forbidden by the law of nature, and is it now established by the special appointment of God, as a law of revelation? Mark! the question is not, Do the Scriptures recognize the relation as established by civil law, and prescribe the duties growing out of the relation thus established? but, Do the Scriptures teach us that it was primarily, or, if you please, at the time of its origin, appointed by God, and intended as an essential and permanent rule or principle of his moral government? If we admit this supposition, does it not amount to an impeachment of the wisdom and goodness of the Creator, in the order of things first established, and thus involve in contradiction and darkness His character and administration, of whom it is said in the Scriptures, "that He is without variableness or shadow of turning," and that "he is light, and in him is no darkness at all?"—a sacrifice too great for the sake of a principle, at best doubtful in theory, and in its general consequences, physical, mental, moral, social, and religious, to both master and slave, of confessedly injurious practical tendency. To give up the lovely character of God, and the confidence we have in the stability and rectitude of his government, as equal in its operations to secure the present and eternal welfare of all his intelligent and accountable creatures, for the sake of sustaining it, is, in the language of poor Richard, "paying too dear for the whistle."

But it is claimed that the Bible recognizes the principle, and adapts its instructions suitably to the relation. Granted. But does it necessarily follow that God, as the moral Governor of the world, has, by so doing, so stamped it with the seal of his approbation, as to vindicate its claims to be an institution of his own appointment? That the Divine toleration, in view of principles and circumstances which will be subsequently pointed out, is lent to the practice, is not denied. But that He has ever appointed it, we demand the proof. It is confidently believed that not a single passage of Scripture can be found in its favour, that will entitle it to the character of an institution of God. And for the all-sufficient reason, that by fair implication they teach the reverse: not in those Scriptures which denounce oppression in general, and the oppression of the poor in particular, &c. An inference from these, because of their general application to all sorts of oppression, seems to us to be too far-fetched, though often quoted by preachers, lecturers, and debaters, and relied on as decisive of the question of the Bible against slavery. We have always thought, because of that generality, they were irrelevant, and for that reason, to intelligent and well-informed minds, inconclusive. But we have a passage, which is admitted both by pro-slavery and anti-slavery men generally, if not universally, to relate to slavery, that speaks directly to the point in hand: "If thou mayest be made free, use it rather." 1 Cor. vii, 21. Now if the apostle, in the use of this language, spoke by Divine inspiration, a state of freedom is, according to God the Holy Ghost, preferable to a state of slavery, and as such, by this high and holy authority, we are commanded to prefer, to seek it. Now in the absence of a single passage in all the Bible to designate slavery as an institution of God; while, on the other hand, we have a passage relating exclusively to slavery, which, by the most natural and direct implication, is a negation of the doctrine; and when the whole spirit and general principles of the book of God, together with the law of nature, lift up

5

their united voice against it, as of Divine right, are we not fairly entitled to the conclusion, that the claim has been hastily made, without sufficient examination? And should not those Scriptures which are thought to favour its pretensions be re-examined, and see if they are not capable of a different interpretation? Such is the view we have taken of their import, which we shall now proceed to show.

First: Is it so presented as to involve the same principles of right, fitness, and moral obligation, which stand out with such prominence in the other relative duties inculcated in the Holy Scriptures; and supported in its pretensions with the same weight of authority? This seems to us to be a consideration of some importance, and entitled to our sober regard in this investigation. For if, in the Divine administration, it is to take rank with the other relative duties of society, it ought to be ascertained and authenticated by considerations of equal weight. Not that the injunction, "Servants, obey your masters," is not of obligation, while the relation providentially continues, and, as such, involving a principle of conscience, on the simple authority of Him who made it, and to whom it is "well-pleasing." But has it the same character of permanency, especially in view of the fact, that the same God who said, "Servants, obey your masters," has also said to servants, "If thou mayest be made free, use it rather." If the same loose principle should be applied to the other relative duties of society—such as civil government, the conjugal relation, parents and children, &c.,—we repeat, if a similar passage of Scripture could be found, virtually dissolving, without any fault alleged against the parties, the civil, conjugal, parental, and filial relations, would it not be fraught with tremendous consequences in its practical bearings; and impair, if not totally destroy, the credibility of the Bible as a revelation from God? But who, on the other hand, can or does, for a moment, question its divinity, or practical utility, because it commands the Christian servant or slave, or any other, to prefer liberty to slavery—freedom to bondage?

Lest, however, it should be thought we are taking for granted that which requires proof, let us look into the Scriptures, and see if the discrimination above alluded to, namely, that the relation of slavery is not backed up by the same reasons of right, fitness, &c., which lend their sanction to the other relative duties of life, is sustained by their testimony. And if, on examination, it shall be found that there is a very important difference as to the manner in which these relative duties are enforced, it will be of great weight in sustaining the doctrine of these pages; which, like the ecclesiastical polity of Methodism, is to avoid the extremes on either hand. And, notwithstanding the confident and boisterous claims of the South to the contrary, that is, to the rightfulness of the relation,—and which, it is to be deplored, was, in a qualified sense, conceded by the late lamented Dr. Fisk, in the following language, contained in his "Counter Appeal:"—"The New Testament enjoins obedience upon the slave as an obligation *due* to a present *rightful* authority,"—let us see if a candid and careful examination of the Holy Scriptures will not vindicate and sustain the discrimination above made; namely, that the obligation of the slave to obedience is not, as the other relative duties of life, placed upon the ground of right, but of moral goodness.

And, first, as to the relative duties of civil government.

In reference to civil government: The history of the Jewish nation, as recorded in the Old Testament, is a standing proof of civil government; and, as such, by the appointment of God. That it was regarded as obligatory, and a great blessing, not only to the obedient, but also in a national point of view, may be inferred from the promise, "The sceptre shall not depart from Judah, nor a lawgiver from between his feet, until Shiloh come." Without noticing more particularly what is said on this subject in the Scriptures of the Old Testament, we will quote from the New, Paul to the Romans: "Let every soul be subject unto the higher powers; for there is no power but of God: the powers that be are ordained of God. Whosoever therefore resisteth the power, resisteth the ordinance of God; and they that resist shall receive to themselves damnation. For rulers are not a terror to good works, but to the evil. Wilt thou then not be afraid of the power? Do that which is good, and thou shalt have praise of the same: for he is the minister of God to thee for good. But if thou do that which is evil, be afraid; for he beareth not the sword in vain: for he is the minister of God, a revenger to execute wrath upon him that doeth evil. Wherefore ye must needs be subject, not only for wrath, but also for conscience' sake. For, for this cause pay ye tribute also: for they are God's ministers, attending continually upon this very thing. Render therefore to all their dues: tribute to whom tribute is due; custom to whom custom; fear to whom fear; honour to whom honour." Chap. xiii, 1–7.

"Submit yourselves to every ordinance of man for

the Lord's sake: whether it be to the king, as supreme; or unto governors, as unto them that are sent by him for the punishment of evil-doers, and for the praise of them that do well." 1 Peter ii, 13, 14.

Now these passages, rightly understood, teach the same doctrine. And what is it? Why, "subjection to the powers that be;" that is, to civil government; or, in the language of Peter, the "ordinance of man," (being framed by human skill.) And the reasons for this subjection are,—

1. That civil government is the ordinance of God; "For there is no power but of God; the powers that be are ordained of God."

2. That in resisting civil government, we resist God, it being his ordinance.

3. That civil government is good, to prevent evil, and promote good works,—as conducive to the individual and general welfare.

4. That civil government, being of Divine appointment, and great practical utility, is of penal and moral obligation. "Wherefore ye must be subject not only for wrath, but also for conscience' sake."

It will be observed by the attentive reader, that our subjection or obedience does not rest simply or exclusively on the authority of God, though that is sufficient, but also on the goodness of the ordinance itself; the importance of which we have heretofore seen as necessary to our existence. Man cannot live without society; society cannot exist without government.

We will, in the next place, notice the conjugal or marriage relation. And here husbands are commanded to love their wives, and be not bitter against them; but to treat them kindly, tenderly, &c.; and the reasons assigned in the Scriptures are,—

1. That they are one flesh,—she being at the first taken from his side. Gen. xxii, 21–24.

2. By virtue of the Divine appointment they are to be considered one to the end of time. Matt. xix, 5, 6. And because of this tender and intimate relation, the apostle argues the impropriety of unkind treatment: "For no man ever yet hated his own flesh."

The wife is required to be in subjection to her husband. Such is the Divine command, whenever the subject is spoken of in the Scriptures. And the reasons assigned are,—

1. That she was formed out of the body of the man. Gen. ii, 21–24.

2. That the woman being deceived, was first in the transgression. Gen. iii, 16; 1 Tim. ii, 11–14.

In the parental relation, parents are variously commanded to care for, instruct, provide, and not to provoke their children to anger, lest they be discouraged; but bring them up in the nurture and admonition of the Lord: and the motive brought to bear on this duty is an appeal to the tenderness of parental solicitude for the present and eternal welfare of their offspring: "That it may be well with you and your children forever."

Children are commanded in all things to obey their parents; and the reasons are,—

1. It is right.

2. The first commandment with promise.

3. Well pleasing to the Lord.

The attentive reader will doubtless have observed that in all the relative duties above enumerated, there is an essential right and fitness, found in the very nature of them, that marks clearly their excellence, and commends them to our understanding as wise and good arrangements.

Let us see in the next place if the slavery relation is supported by the same weight of authority.

And first we will quote from Eph. vi, 5–8: "Servants, be obedient to them that are your masters according to the flesh, with fear and trembling, in singleness of your heart, as unto Christ; not with eye-service, as men-pleasers; but as the servants of Christ, doing the will of God from the heart; with good-will doing service, as to the Lord, and not to men: knowing that whatsoever good thing any man doeth, the same shall he receive of the Lord, whether he be bond or free."

Now in this language of the apostle, which is the most complex, and therefore the most difficult, of any to be found in the Scriptures on this subject—hence, requiring more attention in its explanation—it appears to us the following principles are laid down.

1. The servant's obedience to his master.

2. His obedience to his master for the sake of Christ, as the servant of Christ; doing service as to the Lord and not to men.

3. That in doing this service for the sake of Christ, he does a good thing. Not good or right in itself, according to the eternal fitness of things, as are the duties of the relations above pointed out; but in the present disordered state of things, which the providence of God is superintending to the best possible issue, comparatively good, because done for his sake, and on his authority. This seems to us to be the legitimate and natural sense of the passage—the only one to which we can be conducted in its fair and candid examination. But in addition to this, the analogy of Scripture, if we pay any regard to its unity, shuts us up to this interpretation. For if the state or relation

of slavery was intrinsically good in itself, why should those in that condition be exhorted, "If thou mayest be made free, use it rather?" and those who had attained their freedom, commanded, "Be ye not the servants of men?"

In view of the very similar language and sentiment found in the Epistles to the Colossians and Titus, we deem it unnecessary to do anything more than quote them. Col. iii, 22–24: "Servants, obey in all things your masters according to the flesh; not with eye-service, as men-pleasers; but in singleness of heart, fearing God; and whatsoever ye do, do it heartily, as to the Lord, and not unto men; knowing that of the Lord ye shall receive the reward of the inheritance: for ye serve the Lord Christ."

Tit. ii, 9, 10: "Exhort servants to be obedient unto their own masters, and to please them well in all things; not answering again; not purloining, but showing all good fidelity; that they may adorn the doctrine of God our Saviour in all things."

With the passing observation that there is, as above, the same absence of an authenticating principle, naturally growing out of the relation; the whole weight of obligation resting on extraneous, or foreign considerations,—the will of God. "And whatsoever ye do, do it heartily as to the Lord, and not to men;" and, "that they may adorn the doctrine of God our Saviour in all things."

The next passage to which we will call attention, is found in 1 Tim. vi, 1, 2: "Let as many servants as are under the yoke count their own masters worthy of all honour, that the name of God and his doctrine be not blasphemed. And they that have believing masters, let them not despise them, because they are brethren; but rather do them service, because they are faithful and beloved, partakers of the benefit. These things teach and exhort."

Now here the subjection or obedience of the servant is enforced by the same authority as in the passages already quoted,—the will of God,—but with a little change of phraseology,—the former passages requiring it, for its good consequences; this requiring it, to prevent bad ones. "That the name of God and his doctrine be not blasphemed." Heathen masters, by the disorderly conduct or want of fidelity in their recently converted servants, might be led to attribute it to their religion; and thus, becoming unfavourably affected toward it, and its Author, in their blindness, speak evil of the things which they did not understand. For it is a truth, well known to those who have any experimental knowledge of spiritual things, that such is the enmity of the carnal mind to a spiritual religion, that it is ever ready upon the slightest, yes, even doubtful pretexts, to condemn and discard it. And it is to be feared there are not wanting like examples of inexcusable and abandoned iniquity among the semi-heathen of this Christian country, who are stumbling into hell over the innocent infirmities of others. The apostle understood this deception,—this deep evil of the human heart; and therefore the cautionary language of the passage now under consideration.

There is yet another passage which, in this connexion, demands our attention, found in 1 Pet. ii, 18, 19: "Servants, be subject to your masters with all fear; not only to the good and gentle, but also to the froward. For this is thank-worthy, if a man for conscience towards God endure grief, suffering wrongfully." This contains some important suggestions.

5*

1. As above, they are to be in subjection from a principle of conscience toward God.

2. It is admitted, that in that subjection they may have to "endure grief, suffering *wrongfully*," which is said to be "thankworthy," if endured for the Lord's sake.

3. They are encouraged to this duty by the example of Christ; who patiently, submissively, and uncomplainingly, committing himself to him that judgeth righteously, suffered for us, even to the bearing of our sins in his own body on the tree; not that it was due us, as a matter of right, according to the essential fitness of things; but as an expedient, instituted by the boundless benevolence of the Deity, to overcome evil with good. From these explanatory remarks, which we think are the legitimate and obvious sense of the passage, we are entitled to the following conclusions:

1. That they are to be subject, not because it is right in itself, but for the Lord's sake.

2. That though they might have to endure grief, and suffer *wrongfully* in the discharge of their duty, nevertheless, it was

3. Obligatory upon them, on the same principles of moral goodness that were manifested in the redemption of the world by the sufferings and death of our Lord Jesus Christ, who, in this respect, had left them and us an example, that we should follow his steps.

Alarm may here be taken, that in the above remarks we have started a dangerous principle in theology, viz., That a thing not right in itself, may, under a change of circumstances, become allowable; or, in other words, that a thing not originally right—or right according to the first constitution of things—may, under a change of circumstances, in a perfect administration be tolerated, for the sake of its practical utility. Doubtless the subject has its difficulties, though we think not insuperable. And we are aware of the necessity of caution, lest we introduce principles which, by their looseness, may confound all distinction between right and wrong, and thus sap to its foundations the moral government of God. This subject will more properly come up in the subsequent pages, to which the reader is referred for its examination.

We do not wish it understood, in the above remarks on the relative duties of society as now constituted, that obedience, on the part of servants to their masters, is not, during the continuance of the relation, a Christian duty. Such we believe it; and would feel ourselves bound by the high authority of "Thus saith the Lord," so to teach, were we placed in a situation requiring it. But we mean to say, in view of the facts and arguments brought to bear upon the question, drawn fairly, as we think, from the law of nature, reason, and revelation, that it does not possess the same broad seal, and stamp of right and Divinity, that mark the other relations of society; and is therefore indicated to be not a permanent, but a temporary regulation, which, in the providence of God, may, in the language of the apostle on another subject, "wax old, perish, and vanish away."

In this connexion, as it will be a continuance of the argument against slavery, as an institution of God, it may be well to see what account the Bible gives of its origin. The first notice we have of it, that clearly fixes its character as a property relation, is in the seventeenth chapter of the book of Genesis, about A. M. 2107. Men-servants and maid-servants are previously spoken of, but not so as to fix with sufficient clearness the property relation. But in this chapter, those who were bought with his money are distinguished from his own children, and those that were born in his house; so that whatever may have been the true condition of the servants previously named, it must be admitted, that those he had by right of purchase were his property, having been bought with his money. And the manner and circumstances under which it is brought to notice deserve some attention. God is about to renew his covenant with Abraham, and institutes circumcision as the seal of that covenant. He commands Abraham to circumcise, at eight days old, every male child born in his house, and bought with his money; which Abraham obeyed. For we find in the twenty-third verse of this chapter, that "Abraham took Ishmael his son, and all that were born in his house, and bought with his money, (males,) and circumcised them on the self-same day, as God had said unto him." Now is there anything in the language here used, or the nature of the transaction narrated, that affords the most distant intimation that God instituted or appointed the relation of slavery? It seems to us that no torturing, having any reason or probability on its face, can give it such a construction. From the manner in which it is introduced, it doubtless had obtained prior to the time when the right of circumcision was instituted; and may be fairly set down as one of the inventions of men, instead of an institution of God.

And being thus introduced and interwoven as an element of society, the Holy Scriptures, in giving their directions for the regulation of the social and civil state, adapt their instructions accordingly. And it is only in this incidental way, if our memory serves us correctly, that reference is made to it throughout the Scriptures of the Old and New Testaments. Of this the honest inquirer after truth may satisfy himself, by turning to the various passages of Scripture where the subject is spoken of. And how, under these circumstances, and with these facts before us, it can be magnified into the imposing character of a Divinely-appointed institution, we are at an utter loss to conceive. That in view of the weakness of the present state, under the superintendence of a Providence that embraces all worlds, sweeps over all time, and throughout all eternity, it is in the Divine forbearance tolerated, is not denied. And it may prove, for aught we know to the contrary, such a lesson of instruction to all created intelligences, on the exceedingly unnatural and deeply evil character of sin, as to give the most effectual caution against it. And however it may now appear to our contracted vision, and without any thanks to us, it may, as a measure of moral discipline, prove of the most salutary importance, and so appear to us, when His plans of providence and government, as a whole, are developed.

But that it has the Divine sanction, in the broad sense of that term, so as to exalt it to the character of a Divinely-appointed institution, is contradicted by His whole character and government; which we think has been clearly shown, and abundantly proved, in the preceding pages.

PART THIRD.

THAT THE SIMPLE RELATION IS NO BAR TO CHURCH-FELLOWSHIP.

SECTION I.

FROM THE PRINCIPLES OF GOD'S MORAL AND PROVIDENTIAL GOVERNMENT.

Having closed our argument against slavery as an institution of God, we will proceed, in the next place, to the inquiry, Does the Bible authorize the belief, that a man in the relation, or in other words, that a slaveholder, can be a Christian ?—the relation being no bar to church-fellowship.

It will have been observed by the attentive reader, that, in the preceding pages, we have assumed, and endeavoured to show, that the Bible does warrant such belief. And if we have not misinterpreted the passages quoted—which interpretation we have sustained by numerous authorities, the best-accredited and most reputable the Church and the world have produced for centuries—the truth of our position is fairly made out, and the controversy should be at an end. For if, according to the best lights we have, such is the teaching of the Scriptures, on their high and unerring authority, the question is settled: and accordingly here we might let it rest. For if, in the language of St. Peter, there is in the writings of St. Paul, (and others,) according to the wisdom given unto him, some things hard to be understood, which they that are unlearned and unstable wrest unto their own destruction, on them be the fearful responsibility. For is it not to be expected that an administration, involving "the depth of the riches both of the wisdom and knowledge of God, whose judgments are unsearchable, and his ways past finding out," should, in some of its details, elude our utmost vigilance and most enlarged comprehension? Such seem to have been the views of the great apostle to the Gentiles, who is universally acknowledged to be a man of mind and letters; and our highest reason and sober judgment approve his modesty. But there are some men in whose vocabulary you cannot find the words "I can't," at anything, or on any subject. They are "Northerners," and men of like stripe from all other quarters. Of course, we don't mean the venerable Bangs, the Pecks, or our good Brother Stevens, of the Conference Journal; nor anybody else in all creation, of kindred views and spirit.

But a regard for honest minds in the pursuit of truth, which are perplexed on account of a supposed difficulty in reconciling the relation of slavery with the government and character of God, prompts us to give the subject a little further attention. In doing which, to avoid, as far as we may, confusion of thought in the investigation of a complicated question, we deem it necessary to make the following preliminary discriminations:—

1. That we are not contending for the Divine right of slavery, against which we have entered *our* veto in the preceding pages.

2. Nor yet for the original act of aggression; by which a freeman is reduced to a state of bondage, by whatsoever method accomplished; but

3. When it comes in as an element of organized society, hedged about with the legal encumbrances that are thrown around it, and has passed into hands, by testament or otherwise, that had nothing to do with the original act of reducing them from a state of freedom to a state of bondage, nor the enactment of those laws by which the relation is created, regulated, and perpetuated,—it is tolerated. For the sake of clearness we repeat, that under the circumstances above stated, all else being right, it is tolerated, without prejudice to the creditability of the Christian profession of those thus connected with it.

The principle before alluded to, here involved, is: that the Divine administration, in tolerating the relation, under the circumstances, and to the extent above stated, connives at and lends its awful sanction to sin; and that thereby its essential purity and rectitude are implicated, and the lovely character of God, as the "righteous Lord who loveth righteousness," is given up. But we are not satisfied that this conclusion can be legitimately drawn from the premises. Under the Adamic covenant,—or a rule of simple, rigid, unbending law—it would have to be admitted. But we are not now under an administration of pure, simple law: and well for us that we are not, "for by the deeds of the law there shall no flesh [pro-slavery or anti-slavery] be justified in his sight:" for the all-sufficient reason, that pure or simple law,—or law in the abstract, only makes known the evil of our condition as sinners, ("by the law is the knowledge of sin,") and makes no provision for our deliverance. Hence the nervous language of the apostle above quoted, that "no flesh can be justified by its deeds;" and for these good and valid reasons :—

First. That by transgression, the first covenant or law was forfeited; and,

Secondly. As the result of that transgression, "the mind became carnal,—not subject to the law of God, neither indeed can be;" and hence absolutely incapable of any obedience, let alone the perfect obedience the law required. Prior to that transgression, and the withering, ruinous, and desolating effects brought in its train, "when our reason was clear and perfect, unruffled by passion, unclouded by prejudice, or unimpaired by disease or intemperance, the task would have been easy and pleasant;—we should have needed no other rule. But every man now finds the contrary in his own experience, that his mind is corrupted, and his understanding full of ignorance and error." Hence the alternative was either to suffer the race to perish in that ignorance, error, and corruption, or superinduce on the original plan of government and providence principles to meet the exigency of the case; which, in their operation, while, by reason of their fitness and moral goodness, they preserve unblemished the character of God, as the Moral Governor of the world, and the essential rectitude of his government; at the same time vindicate the righteousness of the Divine administration in their adoption, as an act of boundless condescension to the wants and weakness of man. To the honour and glory of God be it published and proclaimed, from the rivers to the ends of the earth, that our babbling race may know, that in the sufferings, death, resurrection, ascension, and intercession of Jesus Christ, his Son, he has made this provision for us. For the apostle, Romans iii, 21–26, tells us: "But now the righteousness of God without the law is manifested, being witnessed by the law and the prophets: even the righteousness of God, which is by faith of Jesus Christ; whom God hath set forth to be a propitiation, through faith in his blood, to declare his righteousness for the remission of sins that are past, through the forbearance of God. To declare, I say, at this time, his righteousness, that he might be just, and yet the justifier of him who believeth in Jesus." And further; Romans viii, 3–4: "The law of the spirit of life in Christ Jesus has made me free from the law of sin and death. For what the law could not do, in that it was weak through the flesh, God sending his own Son in the likeness of sinful flesh, and for sin condemned sin in the flesh; that the righteousness of the law might be fulfilled in us, who walk not after the flesh, but after the Spirit." Several things of importance to the point in hand are here stated:—

1. That God has superseded the covenant of works, by making faith in Christ the condition of our justification.

2. That the propitiatory sacrifice of Christ Jesus vindicates the rectitude or righteousness of the Divine administration, in the superinduction of this new feature of his moral government.

3. The object to accommodate his dispensations to the unfortunate circumstances of our fallen condition; or, in other words, a gracious stoop in the divine administration to the "weakness of the flesh," which simple law, or the law of works, by reason of its unbending nature, could neither tolerate nor provide for.

4. That this act of moral goodness, manifested in the gift of his Son for the purposes above stated, is a

settled part of his plan of government: "being witnessed by the law and the prophets, the rites and ceremonies of the one, and the preaching and predictions of the other."

In this connexion, we claim the indulgence of the reader for a passing remark, lest some into whose hands this work may fall, should be misled by the terms "boundless condescension," and "gracious stoop," just used. We do not mean, in the use of such terms, to detract from the moral glory of the Divine character and government, for the truth is, in coming down, they went up. For the exhibition of moral goodness in the doctrine of Christ crucified for the sins of the world, is the most luminous and attracting manifestation of the Divine benevolence, and surpassing glory of his moral government, ever made to an intelligent universe.

> "Here the whole Deity is known,
> Nor dare a creature guess
> Which of the glories brightest shone,
> The justice or the grace."

But to return. The term "weakness of the flesh," is one of very extensive import, involving all those direct and remote consequences of sin found in the character and history of man, personally, socially, and civilly, and which mar the beauty, and impair the glory of God's moral system. Now it is to this state of things, and not merely to man as an individual, that the merciful provisions of this new feature of God's moral government apply, adapting themselves to the various conditions in which men, as individuals, or in their social and civil relations, are found. To deny this, is to reject the Divine testimony, that "where sin abounded, grace did much more abound;" and indeed the entire volume of revelation, which is an address, not only to man as an individual, but to men in their social and civil relations. To admit it, is to concede the principle in controversy; for the patriarchal, Mosaical, and gospel dispensations, all found men in this relation, as the reader will have seen in the preceding pages; and of the truth of which he may fully satisfy himself, by a careful perusal of the Holy Scriptures. Now, such being the fact, what is to be done with those persons who, under a providence which "determined the bounds of their habitation," are born, educated, and enter upon the business of life in connexion with this relation, and who were as innocent of the circumstances which originally introduced it, as they were of the sin of Adam? Must they, indiscriminately, be sent to hell? or might they not have been, with as great a show of justice, sent there for the sins of our first parents? or where would be the difference, so far as principle is concerned, in their being born in hell at the first, as to come into the world under circumstances which, ultimately, must inevitably consign them to perdition? Who can split this hair?

Or will the Judge of all the earth, who knoweth our frailty, and the power of circumstances over that frailty, (evil communications corrupt good manners,) take these matters into the account in the final judgment? It seems to us that the following passage of Scripture settles this matter beyond all controversy. "It is required according to what a man hath, and not according to what he hath not."

And on this principle, what an amount of charity is due to persons who, throughout their whole lives, have been connected with a great evil; and that too, whatever we may think to the contrary, to them, under the real or apparent sanction of religion! If they were heathens, all else being right, we would, at least, suppose their final salvation possible, if not certain. And what sufficient reason have we for departing from the same conclusion, in reference to professed Christians? Our mental and moral powers are given us by our Creator to aid us in the pursuit of truth. The Bible, as a revelation from God, is addressed to these powers. Now, if we sincerely bow to its authority, honestly following out that which our highest reason, aided by the best lights within our reach, determines to be the rule of duty, who will take it upon them to say, that the final salvation of such a one is in jeopardy?

But we are here reminded, that the objection is not to the circumstances of our birth and education, but to the relation as being palpably wrong—contrary to the laws of nature and of revelation. That it is contrary to the original law of nature, is readily admitted. Indeed, we have endeavoured to prove it such. But we are not now exclusively under that law. That it is contrary to the law of revelation, as a temporary regulation, adopted in the exigencies of the case, to meet the "weakness of the flesh," or present disordered state of the world, is denied. For, as we have previously seen, the relation was found in existence, as an element of civil society, at the time when the various dispensations were given; and those dispensations, especially the gospel, recognize civil government in this matter as the supreme rule of duty, by enjoining the particular and reciprocal duties arising therefrom. That the Divine government, in the adoption of this measure, connives at, or lends its sanction to sin, as the objection supposes, is by no means clear and satisfactory. For as we have seen, it is not, and could not be conducted on principles of unbending law only in the destruction of the race, "for all had sinned," and therefore all must die. It proceeds therefore on terms of grace, and seeks, on this principle of accommodation to the "weakness of the flesh," to make the best of circumstances for accomplishing, as a whole, the greatest amount of good.

Now in view of the very extensive prevalence of slavery in the world—with the state of things it engendered—impatience of restraint and discontent on the one hand, and pride and ambition on the other, a question arises as to the policy of the Divine administration in managing it for the greatest good of all concerned. This is the rule. Moral goodness, as its ultimate object, is its Alpha and Omega—its beginning and its end.

And that by this measure of policy, or expediency, to secure, under the circumstances, the greatest amount of moral goodness, there is, in the Divine administration, no conflict with the principles of justice and holiness, is obvious. Otherwise, the Divine Being would have been so straitened in the circumstances of a fallen world, as to have prevented its redemption by the death of his Son. It is exactly the same principle in the one case as in the other—an expedient of Divine goodness to make the best of circumstances. And that such an administration is consistent with the character and perfections of the Deity, will appear from the following considerations:—

1. That sheer justice, on principles of essential right, cannot demand perfect rectitude of those who, under circumstances over which they had no control,

are so impaired or perverted in their mental and moral powers, as to be absolutely incapable of the rule. To contend otherwise, is to unsettle and confuse, if not entirely destroy, all our conceptions of right and wrong; and also to shut up the Divine administration, as the only alternative to the cutting off the race in our first parents. For it cannot be reconciled with the perfections of the character and government of God, to suffer through them, and by their fault, the existence of an intelligent and accountable race, under the influence of a moral taint that totally disqualifies them for perfect original obedience, and then damn them to all eternity for want of such perfect obedience.

2. If, then, through them, in their fallen condition, as the progenitors of mankind, it was just to continue the race in existence, the very same justice required that a benevolent regard should be had to the circumstances under which they were to exist. For instance, as before observed, for us, in the providence of God, to be brought into existence in connexion with this evil; and our education, from birth to manhood, be such as to impress us with the rightfulness, or at least the comparative innocence, of the system; and further, for the force of those educational impressions to be strengthened by the overawing tendency and paramount authority of Divine revelation, in the rules of moral duty therein laid down for the government of the relation, as an element of the social and civil state; and the frequent tolerant allusions found to such a relation;—and connected with this, for it to be absolutely impossible for any man to give any plausible exposition of these passages as a whole, level to the common apprehension, that would exclude the relation from the Scriptures, as one of Divine toler-

ance or forbearance ; and for it to be generally known, on the other hand, to be the opinion of the wise, pious, and exemplary of mankind, that the Scriptures do recognize and teach the duties of such a relation ; and the whole question to be additionally embarrassed by the solemn forms and sanctions of municipal law ;—we repeat, that if it is just to continue the race in existence under such circumstances, the very same justice requires that a benevolent regard be had to those circumstances; otherwise the principle is involved that we sometimes hear eloquently and pathetically urged by certain agents of missionary and Bible societies, to induce the people to be liberal in the support of those very worthy objects, namely, that the heathen are damned in mass, simply because they are heathen; no other fault being alleged but that which must necessarily grow out of heathenism—a want of the Scriptures. We remember recently to have been present at one of these meetings, in the town of Seneca ville, Ohio, and to have heard one of the agents of the American Bible Society take this ground. He stated, in round numbers, that there were eight hundred millions of heathen in the world, and that this number gave a ratio of mortality of seventy-five thousand per day, who all, without let or hindrance—men, women, and children—were going down to hell, for the enormous crime of being born, living, and dying in a state of heathenism. Gracious Heaven! thought we, if this be a fair representation of the essential character of God as taught in the Bible, the less of Him and his Bible that can be known, the better! For, if this be a fair representation of His goodness, justice, and mercy, wherein does it differ from the most essential malevolence and tyranny?

It is to this grave aspect of the question, as involved in the doctrine controverted in these pages, that we enter our solemn protest.

It must be, then, that in the Divine administration a benevolent regard is had to the circumstances of our existence; and that regard was manifested in the atoning sacrifice of our Lord Jesus Christ; which, while it clearly marks the deep evil of sin, by exhibiting, in the sufferings and death of the Son of God, its awful deserts, in an administration of perfect rectitude, effectually guards our conceptions of the essential purity and holiness of God, as the moral Governor of the universe; and, at the same time, gives such an affecting display of moral goodness, in the intense solicitude manifested for the welfare of his erring children, as to commend the whole transaction to our admiring, adoring, and grateful wonder, that His infinite resources were equal to the emergency. So that it manifestly appears, that a regard for circumstances, in reference to the relation of slavery, instead of being an impeachment of, is perfectly consistent with, the rectitude of the Divine government.

And what were those circumstances? As above intimated, slavery was very general throughout the world; and a deeply-rooted jealousy and vigilance, in both parties, marked the history of its existence. Under these circumstances, to have attacked it, and by direct, positive precept forbid it, would have been the signal for universal civil revolution, war, and bloodshed, in which the very name of Christianity would have become odious beyond endurance, and every vestige of it lost in the general uproar and confusion. This, probably, is the very reason why a different course—even the one contended for in these

6

pages—was adopted, which, while its practical utility inspires public confidence, operates to the subversion of the principle, by the real moral improvement of both master and slave; for it is confidently believed, that the full development of the principles, spirit, and power of Christianity, in all the ramifications of the present state, would cause it to vanish away. But that state of things, in the providence of God, and the onward march of Christianity, has not yet arrived.

Its power, as bearing more directly on civil polity, has been felt in the British government; and the moral triumph has been worthy of the source from whence it emanated. The difficulties to be encountered there were feeble, in comparison of those in the United States, it (African slavery) having never obtained, so as to become connected with, and interwoven in the social and civil state at home, being chiefly confined to their distant colonies and plantations.

Its power has also been felt in the United States, confined, however, principally to the individual and social circles; and as the result of its bloodless achievements, one million, or thereabouts, out of the three millions of our coloured population, have been emancipated—delivered from their yoke of bondage. Nor has it been altogether inefficient in its silent but powerful appeals to the powers that be: as the Saviour of mankind knocks at the sinner's heart, it has long been standing at the door of civil authority, knocking for entrance; and, as with Him too generally, those in high places have been either too busy or too merry to give heed to the voice without.

Recent developments, however, indicate a favourable change. It has gained a hearing in the courts of some understandings among those in high places; and, vindicating successfully the eternal rightfulness of its claims, has obtained from conscience, the "vicegerent of God within us," or the supreme judge in this court, a favourable verdict; and through their influence (some of whom have fallen asleep: honour to their memory!) has at length got into court. With various success, its friends have been urging its claims for years; each renewed effort has increased their numbers, until their thickening ranks, at least in some aspects of the conflict, have given them the ascendency. And now this silent voice of moral power not only fills the court-rooms, (Senate and House of Representatives,) but, as an earthquake-shock, its power is being felt from the Atlantic to the Pacific, from the Lakes to the Gulf;—the whole nation is aroused: and may Heaven speed the right, until a nation's throes (including the States concerned) shall civilly bring forth fruits meet for repentance, by "breaking off every yoke, and letting the oppressed go free."

Till this be done, if we have read our Bible correctly, the relation—in the absence of the power of the Church to control, by moral principle, the power of the State—may lawfully continue, or, if you please, continue on Bible principles. No carnal weapons—not even the infraction of existing civil law, only so far as it can be effected constitutionally, orderly, peacefully, by the power of moral principle—are admissible in this passionless war of moral power. To every other weapon, movement, or emotion, Jesus, in the principles and spirit of the Gospel, says, as he said to Peter on another occasion, "Put up thy sword."

It will doubtless be objected by many, that we invest the civil with too great a control over the spiritual power. We are fully aware that this is a point of great delicacy in this investigation; and that great caution is necessary to guide us safe from the rocks on either hand. The Bible, however, is our chart and compass; and following its directions and indications, we shall be conducted to safe moorings.

It will be remembered by the reader that we have, in the preceding pages, made allusions to this question, in which we have taken the ground that the civil power is the supreme rule of duty to the State and to the Church, collectively and individually; and is binding in the court of conscience, when it does not conflict with the law of God. If, as in the case of Daniel, or the three Hebrew children, it comes in direct contact with, or contravenes the Divine law, in all such cases it is our duty to "obey God rather than man," and endure the consequences; "committing the care and keeping of our souls to him in well doing, as unto a faithful Creator." Resistance to civil authority is not justifiable, on pretended or real principles of conscience, in any case of doubt. It must be clear beyond doubtful disputation, otherwise we fall under the condemnation of those who resist the ordinance of God.

It may here be urged that religious bodies have, under the tolerating principles of this government, the right to organize on such principles as to them appear to be the most agreeable to the word of God, and as shall, in their judgment, be the best calculated to promote the interest of the Redeemer's kingdom. Granted. But this is not the question in controversy. It is, whether the relation of slavery is, on the principles of the Bible, in the present state of society, a bar to Christian communion. That a religious body may organize,—making the relation a bar to church fellowship,—is not denied. But that they are sustained in such action by the authority of the Holy Scriptures, is an unwarranted assumption, contradicted by the various passages we have quoted, and to which the reader's attention has been called.

And furthermore, while, as we have seen, both the Jewish and apostolic Churches admitted such persons to their fellowship, it is confidently believed that not one single passage of Scripture can be found in all the Bible, which, when properly understood and interpreted, according to the analogy of faith, or the principles and spirit of the law of revelation, requires on this question the action of the Church, in advance of the action of the State, nor by consequence individual action in emancipation, in advance of the action of the State, as a condition of salvation, at least, till they have made a fair effort for constitutional redress.

The alarm of heterodoxy may be here sounded; and if we had more regard for our reputation than we have for our honest convictions of truth, or what we regard as the Bible view of this question, we might, could we have reconciled it with our convictions of duty, have passed it without notice. But believing that "truth is never indebted to a lie," on this or any other subject, we have made this frank avowal of our sober convictions.

That good men, from a principle of moral goodness, which will be approved by conscience, may emancipate their slaves and do a good work, especially if they improve their condition by so doing, is not denied. Nor yet that good men have been impelled, from a fear of the pains of future wrath, to manumit their servants; but that those fears have arisen from a well-instructed conscience, fully illuminated by the blaze of inspiration, flaming out in the word of God, may be honestly doubted, for the plain and obvious reason that our duties under the Divine administration can never clash. That the principles of moral goodness inculcated in the gospel may, and will, lead us to embrace every practicable opportunity to do this sum of good to those in bonds, is fully believed. But that it can be required as a principle of conscience, in contravention of existing civil law, as a doctrine of the Bible, is an assumption that needs to be proved.

Of course these remarks have reference to those states where deeds of manumission will not be admitted to record, and which appear to us to be sustained by the following reason:—They are known in law only as a slave or servant,—the property of an owner, and as such, in the person of the owner, these laws, though far too feebly, throw the dim shadow of their protection over him. Whereas, if you emancipate him, he is thrown without the protection of all law; because, in a civil sense, he has no existence only as a slave. Therefore, in liberating, you entirely outlaw him, which, I presume, is a worse condition than to be in the hands of an owner so humane as would liberate him, could he do it to the servant's advantage. And we suppose the gospel of our Lord Jesus Christ not only does not require, but positively forbids our worsting any man's condition as a whole. This is the rule.

And these civil or municipal laws, just so far as they were made and are continued, for the purpose of binding down in mental and moral degradation, and thus regulating and perpetuating the system of American slavery, however they might have passed in the darker ages, are, in the present state of society, the outstanding and unmistakable notices to an intelligent universe, of the deep moral ignorance and deeper inhumanity of the times that originated them, and of the people among whom, and emphatically so far as, they now practically exist.

And it may here be observed, although as we have conceded, and as it must, we think, be conceded by all reasonable men, that a precedent is found in the Patriarchal, Jewish, and Christian Scriptures for the relation, and the duties belonging thereto, where it was established as an element of civil society at the time they were respectively given; they at the same time afford no precedent whatever for the degrading, debasing, crushing, and imbruting laws, which characterize the system of American slavery. This will be seen in the subsequent pages, where it is clearly shown, that under those dispensations its tolerant recognition is guarded and restricted, to the good of the slave; not as a brute, or mere beast of toil and burden, but as a man, in his mental, moral, and religious culture. Correction is spoken of in the law of Moses; such as we give our own children, with "rods," not with cow-hides, burning irons, bowie knives, blood-hounds, or muskets. And just so far as these have obtained, they are an outrage to humanity, an insult to High Heaven, and a published and proclaimed determination, before an intelligent universe, to defy and set aside His authority.

And in view of these matters, a question of great delicacy and overwhelming interest to the Church comes up, which is, in the execution of the great commission, "Go ye into all the world and preach the gospel to every creature," how far she is to regard these laws. To ascertain, and clearly fix the duty of the Church on this subject, we will propose another question. Do these laws, by heavy penalties, prohibit the mental, moral, and religious culture of the enslaved portions of the community, and thereby directly interfere with, nullify, and virtually, if not positively, give the go-by to the imperious command of Jesus Christ, contained in the great commission above quoted? And if so, what is the duty of the Church? Is it, for fear of the wrath of man, to abide these laws in ignoble silence? Did the Hebrew children do so? Did Daniel do so? Did the apostles of our blessed Lord, in carrying out that great command, and who suffered stripes, imprisonment, and death, in obeying God rather than man, do so? Let the future history of the proud courts and trembling thrones of Nebuchadnezzar and Darius answer; let the waning, struggling, expiring throes of corrupted, but truth-smitten Judaism, and the distracted convulsions of heathen Rome, testify to the issues of this moral conflict. Truth then triumphed, and will again triumph. For the same immutable Jehovah rules. Then go thou and do likewise.

But it is claimed these laws are necessary to the system. Then they are so many speaking-trumpets from the Throne Eternal, of the essential and unmeasured wickedness of the system; as well as reasons of Alpine strength, and length, and breadth, and depth, and height, why it should be the most speedily abandoned that is practicable, in view of the general good.

But it is further objected, that such a course on the part of the Church will endanger the safety of society. It is answered: when the security and peace of society, by a system of unjust, oppressive, and cruel laws, demand the annulment of the law of God,—revoking the great commission of Heaven's mercy to those for whom, above all, it was intended,—the outcast, down-trodden, and neglected masses of society,—("the poor have the gospel preached unto them,")—it is bought too dear. It cannot be done by the Church, without the basest and greatest possible recreancy of duty, and positive high treason to the government of God. These are not the vagaries of a distempered imagination, but the sober deductions of reason and truth. Admit the premises, which none can or dare deny, and the conclusion is inevitable. As infallibly, irrefragably, and plainly so, as that one and one make two.

Mark! we have not stated, nor do we, while the relation providentially continues an element of the civil and social state, believe it to be the duty of the Church, in her organized capacity, to touch it in any other way than by inculcating the particular and reciprocal duties arising therefrom, as taught in the Christian Scriptures. We disclaim all such interference, as being incompatible with her subordinate position. We only array her against these laws; and that just so far as they, under severe penalties, prohibit the mental, moral, and religious culture of the slave, and thereby contravene the direct command of Christ,—"Go ye into all the world, and preach the gospel to every creature,"—and in so doing set at defiance the authority of Heaven. Rather than submit to this, let the Church, in the name, and trusting in the strength of the Hebrew children's God, Daniel's God, Peter and the other apostles' God, and the God who has said, for the encouragement of his disciples in all future ages, "Lo, I am with you alway, even unto the end," gird herself to the conflict, and go forth into this black field, "white unto the harvest," and tell these oppressed captives their high origin, vast capacities, and higher destinies through grace, if they will only knock under to the claims and reign of the blessed Jesus, who came "to bind up the broken-hearted, proclaim deliverance to the captives, and the opening of the prison to them who are bound;" and who, in pursuance of this object, laboured, suffered, died, rose; and thus, triumphing over principalities and powers, at last ascended into heaven, to appear in the character of the world's High Priest before the throne of God, making intercession for us and them. We repeat: Let her buckle on the "armour of righteousness on the right hand and on the left," and go forth, as God commands, "to preach the gospel to every creature." What if, in the onset, a few Shadrachs, Meshachs, and Abed-negos, are cast into the burning fiery furnace, or Daniels into the lions' den, or Peters, Pauls, Silases, and their coadjutors, are cast into prison, and finally put to death? The truth will finally triumph. And if the thrones of Chaldea, Babylon, Judea, and Rome, do not tremble to their foundations under the workings of its mighty power—these more notoriously and palpably treasonable insults to God and humanity will soon fall before its onward and conquering march.

And this prediction is virtually already more than realized, in the language of Dr. William A. Smith, of Virginia; who has said in substance, that the Methodist Episcopal Church in that State has power enough to crush the whole system. We are slow to believe it; but would at the same time hope that it is even so; and that she will, in a scriptural and rational way, forthwith harness herself for the battle.

And first, as an organization, if it be necessary, resist unto blood and death, at the post of moral and religious duty, ("committing the care and keeping of their souls to God in well-doing, as unto a faithful Creator,") those laws, if they really do exist, which forbid the mental, moral, and religious culture of the slave; with which, in the days of our boyhood, ourself, in conjunction with others, were threatened, and which operated to break up a Sabbath-school designed for their instruction.

And, secondly; as citizens, having the political power of the commonwealth, by such amendments of the constitution and laws of the State as shall blot forever from the escutcheon of their future history all the ignoble traces of this wretched system, at once their own, humanity's, and the reproach of God.

We feel for and sympathize in its wounded honour. It is our native State. We love its mountains; we love its hills; we love its rocks; we love its valleys; we love its groves; we love its streams,—over, through, among, and along which, we gambolled in all the sportive innocence and gayety of youth; in which we were born, and, with adoring gratitude we name it, "born again"—and to which, in our expatriation, we have often thought of again returning;—and as often as we have thus thought, has the spectre of slavery—this charm and spell of the devil, in which our native State is bound—started up in hideous, frightening, repelling forms before us, in the shape of legal, moral, and social barriers, more unsurpassable and impenetrable than its rivers, groves, and valleys; stronger than its rocks, and higher than its hills and mountains. If he can, may God have mercy, and grant the needful aid.

That the pure and holy religion of the blessed Jesus, taught and enforced in the Holy Scriptures, when properly understood in all its practical bearings, will lead, yea, impel us, from a principle of conscience, to use our influence in a constitutional, orderly, peaceful way, to remove the existing legal impediments, and thus prepare the way of the Lord for the achievement of this moral triumph, is fully believed. And we know not how to reconcile a contrary course on the part of professing Christians, unless it be that they, on this subject, by reason of the dense cloud that hangs over the path of duty, in the shape of conflicting opinions which have darkened counsel by words without knowledge, together with the "ways and means" whereby to make emancipation a boon to them, are so bewildered as only to "see men as trees walking." We hope, however, before we get through this little work, if we can be pardoned for our seeming egotism, to reflect so much light—or perchance more modestly, as well as more appropriately, so to concentrate on the path of duty the rays of light which break upon our mental and moral vision, from the blaze of God's inspiration, that, to keep up the figure, if we shall not now "see every man clearly," we may so far prepare the way of the Lord on this subject, that some more able pen may step forward, and so trace it out, step by step, that the "wayfaring man, though a fool, need not err therein."

These legal obstructions must first be removed. For, after all the big guns, little guns, and pop-guns, that have saluted our ears, on the duty of the Church to take high ground, making slavery a bar to communion, in contravention of existing civil law, we repeat, where is your Scriptural authority for so doing? It is answered: Manstealing is forbidden in the Scriptures—slavery is manstealing—therefore to be rejected by the Church. This assumption has already been sufficiently refuted. Again: oppression in general, and oppression of the poor in particular, are condemned in the Scriptures as unchristian. Admitted. But, as before observed, these terms are of general application to all sorts of oppression; and, from that consideration, insufficient to determine this controversy, especially in the face of a specific law tolerating it.

But in the fifty-eighth chapter of Isaiah we are commanded to "unloose the heavy burdens, let the oppressed go free, and break off every yoke." This is also admitted. But the question here is: Does it, when properly understood, support the doctrine of non-slaveholding as a condition of church-membership? We know it is paraded with all confidence, as decisive of the question. And also, that in some directions a man will risk his reputation for sanity, and be regarded rather as a fit subject for the lunatic asylum, than as an expounder of the word of God, if he questions the soundness of the construction. Nevertheless, we must incur the fearful responsibility, by challenging the correctness of the interpretation, and positively claiming it in support of the doctrine of these pages. The prophet is reproving, in a very severe manner, those addressed, for their mockery and desecration of sacred things. And if the charges brought against them were true, they richly merited the withering rebukes administered. But the question here comes up, who is addressed? To whom does the language, "Let the oppressed go free, and break off every yoke," directly apply? Was it to the non-slaveholding members of the Church? This, as it appears to us, as its true and legitimate sense or meaning, should be fairly made out by those who claim it in support of the doctrine that the relation is a bar to church fellowship. But is such its import? Can any man of common sense, with one grain of candour about him, answer in the affirmative? We think not; and that for the plain and obvious reason, that the context, beyond all controversy, settles it otherwise. It is addressed to the Jews as a nation, as the reader may see, by referring to the first and second verses of said chapter; in which capacity they were guilty of the oppressions here charged against them, and which, as a nation, they were commanded to put away. To illustrate it:—Suppose this government, which has basely (though we hope without due reflection) connived at and lent the weight of its sanction and protection to African slavery and the slave-trade, from which as yet it has not washed its hands, should proclaim a fast, having no reference to humiliation or repentance for its blood-guiltiness in this matter; the language of the prophet—"Is not this the fast that I have chosen, to loose the bands of wickedness, to undo the heavy burdens, and to let the oppressed go free; and that ye break off every yoke"—would apply in all its force. And should the nation hear and obey the language of the prophet, "and bring forth fruits meet for repentance," by removing all those legal obstructions which it has thrown around the relation, and do all in its power to repair its own wrongs to bleeding Africa,—and should the

Southern States nobly follow in this illustrious example, the way would be open for church and individual action, as indicated by the prophet in the seventh verse. So that the most natural construction of the passage gives no countenance to the new measures, into the service of which it is sought to be pressed; but the contrary, as the reader will have just seen. And it may be confidently affirmed, that it is only by such perversions and misapplications of the sacred text, together with a total misconception of the relation, as connected with the moral and providential government of God, that they can derive any support from the Holy Scriptures.

SECTION II.

ITS COMPATIBILITY WITH THE RECTITUDE OF THE DIVINE CHARACTER AND GOVERNMENT.

But we have not yet done with it. Having shown, as we think, on the authority of the Holy Scriptures, that the relation is, in the sense, and to the extent, stated in the preceding pages, tolerated in the Divine forbearance, as a principle of his moral and providential government, we will now proceed to show its compatibility with the rectitude of the character and administration of the moral Governor of the universe. As already seen, this is by many regarded as a hopeless task. We frankly admit that it has its difficulties, though we think not insuperable. A careful perusal of the sacred page will illumine our pathway, and conduct us to satisfactory conclusions. For if the principles, reasonings, and deductions, contained in the former pages, are drawn from the Bible, as we think they are, and it is consistent with itself, it must reflect light on this complicated question.

It will be remembered, that on a former occasion we laid down the principle, that the remedial dispensations are addressed not only to men as men, but to men in their social and civil relations. We then intimated the soundness of this view, as being involved in the apostle's argument, that the merciful provisions of the gospel are equal, or more than equal to the ravages of sin:—"Where sin abounded, grace did much more abound." And also from the fact that they are addressed to men in their individual, social, and civil capacities. We need not here pause to prove a position so obviously true. The fact is too notorious to require it, further than to say, first, that the gospel is to be preached to every creature,—to all nations,—enforcing their duty not only individually, to God and themselves, but socially, in the relation they sustain to each other, and civilly, as subjects and citizens of the State. And all this as unto God, whose administration sweeps over and takes up all these interests. And second, that the Patriarchal, Jewish, and Christian dispensations, at the time of their announcement, all found slavery as an element of society. This, in the face of the Scriptural authority already introduced, together with the unequivocal voice of history as to the fact of its existence, and the extent of its prevalence, will not, cannot be denied.

That the influence of sin has poisoned and deranged all the departments of our present existence, is too fearfully true to admit of serious or sober doubt. The history of the world, in a voice like the "sound of many waters," proclaims the individual, social, and civil wickedness of the race, as manifested in the abandoned iniquity of private character, social wrongs, and public oppression.

Now the reign of favour, carried out under the Divine government as now constituted, takes hold of, and adapts itself to, this variety, in the exigencies of our present condition, giving those instructions which are suited to that variety—the practical tendency of which, in view of all the circumstances of the present state, are beyond all controversy the most beneficial, and best calculated to promote the general welfare. The fact that such is their tendency with regard to the relation of slavery, is so very apparent in the Scriptures, that it is difficult to conceive how it could have been overlooked, and can only be accounted for on the principle, that we look to our rights under the law of nature; forgetting, at the same time, that the conditions of our primitive existence have been forfeited by transgression, which defaced the beauty and order of God's moral system; and that we are now under a reign of grace, which has relaxed the uncompromising principles of the first covenant, in accommodation to the "weakness of the flesh," and accepts, through the world's Atonement, the best an honest heart, in view of all the providential circumstances of our existence, can perform. We repeat, the want of understanding correctly the principles of God's moral and providential government, as adapted to the present disordered state of the world, is what has misled us in the views we have taken of this intricate question.

To the law and testimony, as the ultimate standard of appeal for the settlement of this question.

Its first mention is in connexion with Abraham, who was commanded to circumcise them, and thus introduce them to the benefits of the covenant of blessing which God had made with him, and through him to all mankind. "And in thee shall all families of the earth be blessed," Gen. xii, 3; and Gal. iii, 8: "In thee shall all nations be blessed." Circumcision was the sign and seal of this covenant; and THEY, in receiving this rite, became interested in its benefits, simply because of THEIR RELATION to his family. Now, was it of no advantage to them thus to partake of God's blessing? Whatever may be the estimate that scoffers at Divine revelation may put upon it, pious minds will be far from admitting it; so that the good practical tendency of the doctrine of the Scriptures, in this first mention of the relation, cannot be for one moment doubted by the believer in the oracles of God.

The next place where we find it introduced to notice, to which we shall call attention, is under the law of Moses, Leviticus xxv, 44: "Both thy bond-men and thy bond-maids, which thou shalt have, shall be of the heathen that are round about you; of them shall ye buy bond-men and bond-maids."

Here it will be seen that the same principles and reasonings apply as under the former, or patriarchal dispensation, noticed in the case of the servants of Abraham. If it was any advantage to enjoy the blessings of the Jewish religion, THEY, as their servants, were in this relation, by virtue of God's commandment, entitled to those blessings.

We will next call attention to the question as found under the New Testament, or gospel dispensation. It comes up under altered circumstances, and therefore requires more particular attention in its examination. Under the dispensations just named, which, as we have seen, though intended in their ultimate development for all the "families" and "nations" of the earth, were confined first to one particular family; secondly, to one particular nation, as the depositories of the true religion. The principle and practice of slavery having obtained, it was comparatively an easy matter, under these circumstances, to restrict it (which was done) to those who, so far as the true religion was concerned, should be benefited, or derive advantages from the relation. But the state of things in the providence of God was greatly changed when the gospel dispensation was announced.

The fulness of time had come, as foretold by the prophets, when the purposes of his mercy in the mission of Christ were to be made known to all nations for the obedience of faith. Accordingly we find the shepherds, while watching their flocks by night on the plains of Bethlehem, visited by an angel, accompanied by a multitude of the heavenly hosts, who said unto them, "Fear not: behold I bring you glad tidings of great joy, which shall be to all people." And in the commission of Christ to his disciples, as recorded by St. Matthew, they were commanded to go and "teach all nations to observe all things whatsoever I have commanded you." Now, as the patriarchal and Mosaical dispensations took hold of the individual, social, and civil relations of a single family or nation, and delivered their instructions, as we have seen, obviously the best calculated to promote the best interests of all concerned, in reference to the eternal state; so the gospel of our Lord Jesus Christ takes hold of all nations, and carrying out the same principle, recognizes the possible Christian character (in the relation) of both master and slave, and adapts its instructions accordingly, with this difference ; that it exhorts the servants, "If thou mayest be made free, use it rather."

In this connexion, it may not be improper to express our opinion as to the import of this inspired injunction. That it is a delicate point, we are fully aware ; and also that it is involved in some difficulties. But as the revelation of God which tolerates the relation is "profitable for doctrine, for reproof, correction, and instruction in righteousness, it is fairly to be presumed that its spirit and principles reflect some light on this aspect of the question. And it is to be remembered, that it is only by taking this general view of the subject, that we can arrive at satisfactory conclusions with regard to it.

With these preliminaries we remark, that whatever else it may mean, it cannot be pleaded in justification of the individual or systematic efforts made and making by persons, either in the free or slave States, to persuade, or by stealth or otherwise effect, the elopement of slaves from their legal owners ; for the obvious reason, that if civil government be the ordinance of God, and the Christian Scriptures, as we have shown, recognize it as the supreme rule of duty in this matter, in so doing we "resist the ordinance of God,"—"do evil that good may come,"—a practice nowhere justified by the Bible. The parable of the good Samaritan, though quoted with great confidence as justificatory of this practice, is entirely irrelevant ; the civil condition of the man who fell among the thieves remaining just the same after, as before, the kind treatment received.

There is another passage found in the book of Deut., xxiii, 15, 16 : "Thou shalt not deliver the servant that has escaped from his master unto thee," &c., which is quoted and relied on with great assurance, as lending its sanction to the above practice; but we think with an equal perversion as in the case of the man who fell among thieves, just noticed. The injunction is addressed to the Jewish nation; the only one on the face of the earth, at the time, that was not idolatrous, and which, as before seen, was the depository of the true religion. Now the fact that this law was delivered to them in their national capacity, is proof positive that it cannot be understood as requiring them to hold or retain each other's escaping servants. The bad practical consequences, so disastrous to the peace of the nation, resulting from such a course, or the infraction of a practice which the laws they received from the mouth of God tolerated, forbids, absolutely, such a construction of the passage; especially in the face of what seems to be its most easy and natural meaning, a sense so consonant with the whole spirit of the patriarchal and Jewish law on this subject; which is, that these escaping servants were from the heathen idolatrous nations round about them, and who, on coming among them, were benefited according to the superior advantages of the Jewish religion, as compared with their former heathen state or condition. We cannot therefore admit the propriety of its being pressed into such service. It cannot be done without doing violence to the plain and obvious sense of the passage, as well as to the whole spirit of the Jewish law.

There are other modes of redress inculcated in the Bible, to which allusion has been previously made.

And while on this subject it may be perfectly in place to say, that the fugitive laws of this General Government, which have been, and are now, felt by the non-slaveholding or free States to be a great injustice and indignity to them, derive no support from this Jewish precedent. Our reasons for this position are various, one of which we will here state; and which is virtually the same we have given why the Jews were forbidden to deliver up to their owners the escaping servants of heathen masters. These servants, as just remarked, were running away from heathenism to Judaism, and by so doing, as a whole, were improving their condition. The "fugitives held to service," or escaping servants of the slaveholding States, are running away from a state of semi-heathenism, to a situation where their privileges and advantages are more favourable to the end of their creation, as rational and accountable beings. Not but what the South has the gospel as well as the North; but the laws which have been made, and in many of those States are still in force, to guard and protect this interest, so crush them, civilly, socially, intellectually, and morally, as comparatively to heathenize them. And as the great law of Christianity is, that, as a whole, we are never to worst any man's condition, these fugitive laws are a nullity, because in violation of that law. God's law is and should be supreme. We need not here quote authorities to make good our position, relative to the verity and iniquitous character of these laws; the facts are outstanding and notorious, to heaven and earth.

We have here made some allusions to the servant's running away from his master. Our views on this subject will be seen in what immediately follows.

Should it be inquired, if the law and spirit of Christianity forbid the kind of interference above stated, how far is it the privilege of the servant for himself, to act upon this injunction? we answer, if we should allow Onesimus to have been a slave, as some contend, the question would be settled by direct scriptural authority. But it is thought by some to be of doubtful authority, and therefore not relevant to the point in hand. Waiving this, we are therefore left to the general principles and spirit of Christianity to determine this question. If we admit, as I think we are bound to do, that in the Divine forbearance, in accommodation to the weakness of the present disordered state, the Scriptures tolerate the relation; the distinct and vigilant manner in which they point out and guard its duties, both to "believing and froward masters," very strongly intimates their Christian obligation to continue in the relation, so long as it is providentially encumbered with legal difficulties; which view is very much strengthened by the following passage of Scripture: "Let every man abide in the same calling wherein he was called. Art thou called being a servant? care not for it." 1 Cor. vii, 20, 21. And the whole question, as it appears to us, is powerfully confirmed by the spirit of Christianity, which proposes to achieve, in a peaceful and orderly manner, all its triumphs, by the principles of moral goodness. That the escaping servant will jeopard his salvation by so doing, we will not take it upon us to say. We simply mean to say, that the course the gospel points out is the more excellent way.

These views, when we entertain correct conceptions of the Divine government, commend themselves to our understanding, as Scriptural and rational; and while treating the subject generally, as an honest man, we cannot suppress them.

But to return. At the time as above stated when

the gospel was announced, the nations of the earth, except the Jews, were all heathen; among whom slavery was general, and indiscriminate as to clime, nation, and colour. The discrimination that guarded and restricted the slavery of the Patriarchal and Mosaical dispensations to the heathen, who, so far as a knowledge of the worship of the true God is a blessing, were benefited by the relation, now became impracticable, for all were heathen. Under these altered circumstances, though we have not, and cannot have, the same light which marked the practical utility of the relation under those dispensations, yet we think it will appear, on a careful examination of the principles, spirit, and teaching of the gospel dispensation, that the same wisdom and goodness that tolerated it under those dispensations, does under it.

We will now observe that the remedial dispensation does not propose, in the absolute sense of the term, to do the best according to the essential and eternal principles of right;—this would be conducting the Divine government on the covenant of works,—"Do this and live,"—in which all our ideas, or conceptions of remedy, would be entirely excluded; and all those overwhelming and attracting exhibitions of moral goodness, displayed in the Divine forbearance, so eminently calculated to subdue and win us back to our proper allegiance, and which are so beautifully and forcibly expressed by the poet,—

> "His love is *mighty* to compel:
> His *conquering* love consent to feel:
> Yield to his love's *resistless* power,
> And fight against your God no more—"

would be lost.

We therefore conclude that it is an expedient superinduced upon the original plan of government, proposing to do the best that can be done under the circumstances. We are utterly unable to conceive of it in any other light. Any other view seems to us necessarily to involve the conclusion, (we speak it with reverence,) that the whole Bible is a solemn farce, —a perfectly unintelligible, unmeaning record. But the Scriptures settle this question. "But now we are delivered from the law, that being dead (the law) wherein we were held; that we should serve in newness of the spirit, and not in the oldness of the letter." Rom. vii, 6. And this in accordance with the settled principles of God's moral government: "For thus it is written, and thus it behooved Christ to suffer," as an expedient of infinite wisdom and boundless goodness, in condescension to the weakness and wants of the present disordered state, "and arise from the dead the third day, and that repentance and remission of sins might be preached in his name among all nations;" from which it distinctly appears that under the Divine government, as now constituted, provision is made for the temporary toleration of a state of things that could not have existed under the original law, or law of nature.

The general spirit of Christianity, as expressed in the following Scripture language,—"It is required according to what a man hath, and not according to what he hath not;" and, "Unto whomsoever much is given, of him shall be much required,"—and the reverse, demonstrably indicates, that the rigid and unbending claims of the original law are relaxed; and that under the reign of mercy, in our common parlance, "the will is taken for the deed;" or in other words, the best that can be done under the circumstances.

Having, as we think, from the general principles

and spirit of Christianity, fairly established it as a doctrine of Divine revelation, that the government of God is conducted on principles of leniency toward us; and that, in view of the "weakness of the flesh," it tolerates a state of things incompatible with the unbending principles of original law; and that this gracious stoop is an act in which the blending glories of His wisdom and goodness lucidly shine forth; let us see if the same wisdom and goodness are not luminously conspicuous in the teachings of the New Testament on the slavery relation.

SECTION III.

AS SEEN IN ITS PARTICULAR AND RECIPROCAL DUTIES.

And, first, as to the particular and reciprocal duties of the relation, and which we think are all summed up or comprehended in the following passages:—"Servants, be obedient to them that are your masters according to the flesh, with fear and trembling, in singleness of your heart, as unto Christ; not with eye-service, as men-pleasers; but as the servants of Christ, doing the will of God from the heart; with good-will doing service, as to the Lord, and not to men: knowing that whatsoever good thing any man doeth, the same shall he receive of the Lord, whether he be bond or free. And, ye masters, do the same things unto them, forbearing threatening: knowing that your Master also is in heaven; neither is there respect of persons with him." Eph. vi, 5–9. "Servants, obey in all things your masters according to the flesh; not with eye-service, as men-pleasers; but in singleness of heart, fearing God: and whatsoever ye do, do it heartily, as to the Lord, and not unto men; knowing that of the Lord ye shall receive the reward of the inheritance; for ye serve the Lord Christ. But he that doeth wrong shall receive for the wrong which he hath done: and there is no respect of persons. Masters, give unto your servants that which is just and equal; knowing that ye also have a Master in heaven." Colos. iii, 22–25; iv, 1. "Let as many servants as are under the yoke count their own masters worthy of all honour, that the name of God and his doctrine be not blasphemed. And they that have believing masters, let them not despise them, because they are brethren; but rather do them service, because they are faithful and beloved, partakers of the benefit. These things teach and exhort." 1 Tim. vi, 1, 2. "Exhort servants to be obedient unto their own masters, and to please them well in all things; not answering again; not purloining, but showing all good fidelity; that they may adorn the doctrine of God our Saviour in all things." Tit. ii, 9, 10. "Servants, be subject to your masters with all fear; not only to the good and gentle, but also to the froward. For this is thank-worthy, if a man for conscience toward God endure grief, suffering wrongfully." 1 Pet. ii, 18, 19.

Now all these passages are kindred in their critical and moral bearings; and we shall forbear further critical remarks than those previously made, at least so far as the duty of the servant is concerned. Our attention is especially called to their moral and practical tendency.

It will be observed that the spirit of all these injunctions is most purely moral, to the exclusion of every other sentiment, passion, or emotion; and is to proceed from the heart, in contradistinction from any outward manifestation of good-will, while there exists a rankling enmity within: and all this as in the sight and under the immediate inspection of the God and Judge of all the earth, whose flaming penetration sifts every corner of the heart, surveying its every thought, as well as comprehending every word upon the tongue. And the obligation is reciprocal, it being as much the duty of the master as the servant to cultivate, from the heart, as in the sight of God, this mutual good-will.

Now the heart being the great spring of human action,—which is deceitful above all things, and desperately wicked; and from which, as a poisonous fountain, flow those bitter streams of moral pollution in the shape of "evil thoughts, murders, adulteries, fornications, thefts, false witness, blasphemies," and all the other wickedness which withers, scathes, and desolates the heritage of God,—is, by the power of Christianity, and the practical tendency of these regulations, changed—the fountain is purified—the tree is made good, and the fruit becomes good. The servant is affectionate and faithful in all his relative duties; and thus inspires the confidence, and conciliates the affection of his master. And the master is to "do the same things," or behave with the same affection and fidelity to the servants, "giving them that which is just and equal."

That the justice and equality here spoken of is that which is due them as servants, or in the relation of slavery, will be remembered to have been the view presented as the opinions of the authorities quoted; which must be of great weight in the absence of any counter exposition, by any author of accredited reputation. In connexion with this, if civil government be an ordinance of God, as we have already seen to be the fact, even as it exists among heathen nations; and if it has established the relation as a part of their political organization, according to the teachings of the Bible, and the principles of the Divine administration, as already explained, it is utterly impossible, while the relation continues, to understand it in any other light.

But it may possibly mean something more. The very comprehensive nature of the terms used—"just and equal"—may indicate, as increasing light shall prepare and point out the way of duty, their obligation to do, as fast as circumstances providentially conspire to that end, the whole good to them that the principles and spirit of Christianity dictate. "Therefore all things whatsoever ye would that men should do to you, do ye even so to them."

Now a relation around which are thrown guards of such high moral and practical utility, and which, as we have seen, is of reciprocal obligation, must necessarily mitigate the condition of the enslaved; while, at the same time, it manifestly improves the condition of both parties. And regulations which, when practically carried out, of unbending or absolute necessity improve the physical, civil, social, and moral condition of the parties concerned, cannot in their character be bad, but the contrary. They, as before intimated, may not be the best of which human nature was originally capable, but in the altered state of our existence, in view of all the circumstances, the best that could be done. Fearless of successful contradiction, we confidently challenge exceptions to the rule.

We go further, and take the ground that the instructions or laws regulating the relation, in the sense set forth in these pages, are, under the circumstances, indispensable to the perfection of Divine revelation as a rule of moral duty; that it would not meet the condition and wants of the world, in its fallen, perverse, and mixed state, without them.

True, the general principles and spirit of Christianity might reflect some light on this subject; but the information necessary to enable us to understand our duty, as derived from these sources, could not be supposed to be sufficiently clear and general to give and authenticate the rule. And, indeed, our natural inaptitude to give our attention to the consideration of duties plainly revealed, accompanied by all those evidences of right and fitness; together with the subjoined motives, which involve our present and eternal interests, is an irrefutable argument in favour of those declared regulations of the Divine government on this subject.

Whatever may have been the origin of slavery, having obtained very generally and extensively in organized society, it becomes a difficult question, not so much to our Maker, as to us, in our weak and mixed condition. Intricately interwoven in the civil and social state; sanctioned and protected by all the solemn forms of law; deriving additional strength from the prejudice of caste and condition; and sustained by the pride, selfishness, and ambition of human nature,—it would appear to have been morally impossible, in view of all the circumstances, for any other course to have been adopted than the one we have marked out in the Holy Scriptures. Heaven, by the omnipotence of our weakness, seems to have been exclusively shut up to this alternative; our history on the subject of this relation, presenting to his moral government an exigency for the Divine forbearance to overcome, similar to the interrupted relations between man and his Maker; and to be overcome by the same principles of moral goodness.

And, as we would naturally expect, from the inimitable and illimitable perfections of the Godhead, the remedy in the latter case makes provision for the former, and is in effect, in both cases, to an intelligent universe, the best, to all intents and purposes, that could be done under the circumstances.

We are delighted to have our views of this subject strengthened by the authority of Dr. Francis Wayland, in his Elements of Moral Science. "This very course which the gospel takes on this subject, seems to have been the only one that could have been taken, in order to effect the universal abolition of slavery. The gospel was designed not for one race, or one time, but for all races, and for all times. It looked not at the abolition of this form of evil for that age alone, but for its universal abolition. Hence, the important object of its Author was to gain it a lodgment in every part of the known world, so that by its universal diffusion among all classes of society, it might quietly and peacefully modify and subdue the evil passions of men, and thus, without violence, work a revolution in the whole mass of mankind. In this manner alone could its object, a universal moral revolution, have been accomplished. For if it had forbidden the evil, instead of subverting the principle; if it had proclaimed the unlawfulness of slavery, and taught slaves to resist their masters, it would instantly have arrayed the two parties in deadly hostility throughout the civilized world. Its announcement would have been the signal for servile war, and the very name of the Christian religion would have been forgotten amidst the agitations of universal bloodshed." Page 214.

How, in view of the facts and principles above laid down, the instructions of the Holy Scriptures for the regulation of this relation, as explained in these pages, can be regarded as an impeachment of the character and government of God, we are at an utter loss to conceive. For it does appear to us, that, under the circumstances, infinite goodness could do no less, and infinite wisdom could do no more.

The principles involved in these particular and reciprocal duties, connected as they are with the general principles and spirit of Christianity, form the best, indeed the only basis of an abolition society, known to, and sustained by the gospel of our Lord Jesus Christ —the great depository of all reforming power. For just in proportion as any system is imbued with, and conformed to, its spirit and principles, is it efficient, or, if you please, almighty to accomplish the benevolent and meliorating objects contemplated,—it being Heaven's great engine of moral power by which to move the world, and move it in the right direction,—from the character of its great Artificer, as a being "in whom is hid all the treasures both of wisdom and knowledge," who may therefore be supposed to know the temper of the materials on which it is to operate, and to possess skill to contrive it according to the most discriminating principles of calculation, for efficiency—and omnipotent power, by which to execute its construction, so as to combine and concentrate fully all the resources of moral energy, that the materials on which it is to operate, according to the laws of their existence, can endure, and essential goodness to set and keep it in operation, for the accomplishment of all its noble purposes, if we will only be co-workers with him, observing the directions given us for working the apparatus of this moral machinery.

All our attempts at improvement, repairs, or mending, will only be the veriest bungling; and we shall always find it the worse for the slightest alteration we may attempt to introduce. Of this we have, or ought to have, if we are not too dull and stupid, or too conceited to learn, indubitable evidence in the fact, that all the tinkering that mankind have done since the creation to improve on their Maker's plans has resulted in failure, and invariably made them the worse for mending, as the abandoned wickedness of the world abundantly proves. And the fact that a larger measure of success has not been realized in our world's history, in this particular direction, is no more objection to its potency for good, than its failure in any other direction. A better devised system to lead men to repentance cannot be conceived. And yet how alarmingly inefficient in the accomplishment of its gracious designs! And so with regard to every other form of evil existing in society. It will, we think, on a critical examination, be found that its ratio of good is about equal in the correction of all the wrongs of earth. There may be some discrepancy, but we think not material. And all that is wanted, is our full and hearty co-operation; that its godlike efficiency and sufficiency may be realized, reversing entirely the present disordered state of things throughout the whole history of our sin-ruined world, by changing us into His own lovely image of moral goodness, "from glory to glory, even as by the Spirit of the Lord."

Then let those who think, or feel, that in the providence of God they are especially called upon to work in the anti-slavery or abolition phases of the present disordered state, organize on these principles. And first of all, let them learn by the operation of these principles on their own hearts, and their power over their own lives, their potency for good, as a qualification, not only to recommend them for their experimental and practical utility, as realized in their own history, but to instruct others in the nature and effects of their operations. And if, after mature and candid deliberation, in looking over the whole field, and examining the question in the light of soberness and truth, (God's truth,) they shall be conducted fairly to the conclusion, that the sunny South is in ignorance of, or without this moral lever, charged with essential divinity, with which to turn the world right side up; let them emigrate to that land of destitution and need, carrying it with them.

For, notwithstanding its tremendous dimensions of moral power, it is portable; a clear, sound head, and a pure, warm heart, will hold it. And availing yourselves of the Book of directions, which you will find on your arrival, you may set it in the full tide of glorious operation. And we think so far from being met with bowie-knives, pistols, rifles, or Lynch law from the churches, or the reflecting portion of the South, you will be hailed with general acclamations of jumping joy, and regarded as messengers of mercy, and the real benefactors of mankind.

From the unscriptural and irrational manner in which the Southern Church and feeling have been goaded in this matter, by our overlooking the providential difficulties that hang around the question, it may be otherwise, but, apart from this, we must confess we are slow to believe it. There may be exceptions to the rule, but, in the judgment of charity, it is to be supposed that they form a very lean minority.

SECTION IV.

AS SEEN IN ITS GENERAL CONDITION.

As to its general condition: "Art thou called, being a servant? care not for it." If on this subject our investigations were bounded by time, or confined exclusively to the present life; although, on finding the doctrine of the Scriptures to be what we have seen it to be, we should be bound, for reasons already explained, to receive it, however staggering or confounding to our faith or reason. For, as previously intimated, it is but rational to suppose, that an administration gotten up, and carried on, according to the depths of the riches both of the wisdom and knowledge of God, should, in some of its details, be beyond our comprehension. Yet when we examine it as in the teaching of the Scriptures, it connects with eternity; light from that quarter, at least to some extent, chases away the gloom which would otherwise becloud our contemplations. For there are a great many things found in Divine revelation, which, to our contracted vision, would amount to great difficulties in God's providential government of the world, if in their examination we should restrict them wholly to the present life.

We use the term providence in its strictly literal sense—"The care and superintendence which God exercises over his creatures."—(*Webster*)—and not in that loose sense which would involve the special and positive appointment of the relation. For it is one thing to appoint the relation, and another, and a very different thing, to take hold of a relation, that the wickedness and the weakness of the world has introduced, in derangement of God's original plan, and superintend it to the best possible issue. This seems to us, if we have not misunderstood the doctrine of Calvinism, to be one of the insuperable difficulties into which the doctrine of foreordination runs;—either wholly contravening God's providential government, or so confounding it with a government of original positive law, as to render it very difficult, if not entirely impossible, to discriminate between them. For if He, from all eternity, "foreordained whatsoever comes to pass," where is there room or play for a providential government; unless we admit the possibility of the certain, unalterable, and eternal decrees of the immutable Jehovah failing, for the want of such vigilant supervision?—a difficulty too into which those must run, who contend for slavery as a special appointment of God, by original or positive laws, which must be fatal to the soundness of the argument. For, as we have already seen, there is nothing to be found in the law of nature, or in all the Scriptures, that can, by any rational construction, be brought in support of its pretensions; while, on the other hand, the whole of them, which are given for the regulation of this relation, can at once, by the most easy and natural construction, be seen to be mere providential regulations for the government of a state of things found in the world at the time of their delivery.

But to return. A providential difficulty found in

Divine revelation, is in the case of Lazarus and the rich man of the gospel, and which cannot be satisfactorily explained by the light of time. How it can consist with an administration of perfect rectitude, for a man of the piety of Lazarus to suffer not only in body, but also for want of the necessaries and comforts of life; while the rich man, who, from his character, as given in the Scriptures, to make the very best of it we can, lived in total neglect of all religion, and made the world his God; and who by the whole weight and influence of his character and example, if not of his precepts also, contributed to that general corruption of morals and of manners, which ever has, and ever must, under the present constitution of things, obtain, when all sense of the Divine character, and our obligations to fear and account to him, are obliterated? We repeat; this case, so far as the present life is concerned, presents quite a difficulty in Providence. For we would very rationally expect, from the nature of the case, as well as from some passages of Scripture, that the full horn of the Divine blessing would have been poured along the pathway of the pilgrimage of Lazarus, as the friend and worshipper of God; and that the rich man would have been, on account of his wickedness, the subject of loathsome bodily affliction, felt the griping hand of poverty, and been carried about as a houseless, homeless wanderer, at once the pity and detestation of mankind. But when we look at it as connected with an eternal state of happiness and misery, the clouds and darkness which hung around it, when examined by the light of time, are at once dissipated; and what was all confusion and mystery before, is now all clear, luminous, and entirely satisfactory. For there is no man in his senses but would prefer the portion of Lazarus as a whole,—embracing time and eternity,—to that of the rich man.

Now, the relation of slavery, as tolerated under the patriarchal and Jewish dispensations, like that of Lazarus, when looked at wholly in the light of time, appears dark and inscrutable. For according to the Scriptures, we, being all equally His offspring, are at a loss to discover the reasons of, or see any good resulting from, this providential regulation of our Maker, in tolerating it. But when we connect it with other facts, standing out with prominence in Divine revelation, namely, that God was selecting a single family or nation to be the depositories of the true religion ;—that prior to that time, in either case, slavery existed ;—and that, in tolerating it, he restricted it to those, and to those only, to whom, in reference to a future state,—or their greatest good, both for time and eternity,—it would be a blessing, the difficulty is at once explained. And what before was all doubt and darkness, now shines forth so clear and luminous, that instead of being longer puzzled at his providential government in this matter, our highest reason approves the measure, and our whole souls are fanned into a flame of devout and grateful adoration, at the blended wisdom and goodness which shine out with such dazzling lustre in this vigilant tact of Providence to educe good out of evil.

Thus far the wisdom and goodness of Providence, as connected with this crooked state of things, that his Satanic majesty, (not our Maker,) aided by his coadjutors in the shape of human beings, had brought about, flames out in such a blaze of glory and goodness, as to be almost dark with excessive brightness.

So much so, that every caviller and fault-finder at His providential dispensations must be forced, with the wondering and adoring apostle, to cry out: "O the depth of the riches, both of the wisdom and knowledge of God! how unsearchable are his judgments, and his ways past finding out," by the utmost stretch of human thought, until he is pleased to reveal them.

But now to the difficulties under the gospel dispensation. We, as formerly, frankly confess, that the altered state of matters and things in general, at the time when the gospel was announced, is somewhat more complex and difficult. For the gospel message was not to a single family or nation, but to all nations; and hence, from the necessity of the case, the relation could not be restricted to a single family or nation. In these altered circumstances, what is to be done? What course is to be adopted? Why, for anything under the whole heavens that we can see to the contrary, the gospel of salvation is to be delivered to them just where and what they are. There seems to us, on the settled principles of the Divine administration, so far as it relates to this subject, to be no other alternative. Either the gospel must be withheld entirely, or partially, or Heaven in mercy (we speak it with reverence) must lump our difficulties, and send his angel to announce to the world "good tidings of great joy to all people." And who dares impeach either the wisdom or goodness, the justice or mercy of the Divine administration, in thus adapting itself to and providing for the best interests of a fallen world; which in its final consummation, in behalf of all, whether barbarian or Scythian, bond or free, is, in the nervous language of the poet,

> "Salvation from sorrow through Jesus's love."

But we are here reminded, that the objection is not to the fact that the gospel was announced to all nations just as it found them, for the obedience of faith, but to its having tolerated the relation. If, as we have seen, and which, when we take into the account the perversion of human nature, must, as we think, so appear to every rational mind, capable of examining the subject in the light of soberness and truth; a contrary course,—one that strikes directly at the evil, by dissolving the civil and social relations of the parties concerned, and thereby arraying them in deadly hostility to each other, involving the world in all the horrors of universal war and bloodshed,—and thus well-nigh, if not entirely, exterminating the race, would have resulted in these consequences; where would have been either the wisdom or goodness, the justice or mercy, of such a measure? In what sense of the word, in view of these natural and inevitable results, growing out of the weakness of the present disordered state, could it be regarded as a dispensation of mercy? In none, we think, whatever. For when we calmly and dispassionately look over the whole ground, taking things just as they were, does it not manifestly appear, that instead of being a just, wise, and good arrangement, or a dispensation of mercy, it would have been one of the most severe inflictions with which the world could have been visited, by the Moral Governor of the universe? Such it appears to us, and must, as we think, so appear to every rational mind. Alarm may be here taken, that in our exceptions to the objection urged—that the gospel ought to have prohibited it—we have included and implicated the principles of justice; we reply:—If, as previously observed, it was just for the Divine Being to suffer the existence of intelligent and accountable creatures under such circumstances, the very same justice requires the exercise of a benevolent regard to those circumstances. And for their ultimate damnation to be determined by circumstances as the necessitating cause, which, in view of the general good, it was better to tolerate, than directly forbid by positive precept, cannot be reconciled with any rational principles of justice of which we can conceive.

But, alas! our world is not rational, nor does it behave rationally. True, this was originally our crowning distinction; but in the pride of our glory we set up for ourselves, forgetting, or not heeding the maxim, "that young folks think old folks to be fools, but old folks KNOW young folks to be fools;" and, as the result, a mental hallucination has "come over the spirit of our dream,"—a cheat has "crept into our faith," which is ever and anon leading us astray. And our reason, which constitutes the man, and which was originally given us to control our animal nature, is dethroned; and by nature the entire race presents to our astonished and confounded vision the heart-sickening, soul-destroying, and God-dishonouring spectacle of the brute running off with the man. And, like all other crazy preople, "we pique ourselves on our inch of wit," and sit in judgment on the counsels of our Maker, instead of receiving the law at his mouth; and rashly conclude, that if the depths of the eternal and incomprehensible wisdom and grace displayed in the scheme of human redemption had been submitted to our maniacal dictation, the plan would have been finished, adequate and complete.

And if this state of things was confined wholly to

the world, among "vain men who would be wise," it would be bad enough; but, in the Church, and among those who aspire to a leadership of the sacramental hosts of God's elect, we have a fearful exhibition of the sentiment of the poet, that some men

> "Would rather reign in hell than serve in heaven."

Thus, we think, we have demonstrably shown, from the settled principles of the Divine government, from the general spirit and character of Christianity, from the teaching of the Scriptures, and from reason, that the Divine character and government, instead of being tarnished by their infinite condescension, in meeting the conditions in which mankind in this revolting province of our Maker's dominions are providentially found, receives an illustration of sublimity, in moral goodness, grandeur, and glory, that may well challenge our babbling earth, from the east, west, north, and south, to triumph with the Psalmist, in the glorious truth, that "The Lord reigneth; let the earth rejoice; let the multitude of isles be glad thereof. Clouds and darkness are round about him;" but "righteousness and judgment are the habitation of his throne:" and, we will add, in view of the interest and confidence that the inhabitants of other worlds may have in the rectitude of his government, let all the heavenly host respond, Amen! and in one loud, long, and eternal peal of praise, shout, "Alleluia; for the Lord God omnipotent reigneth," and not sectarian bigotry.

SECTION V.

THE PERFECT AGREEMENT OF THE ECCLESIASTICAL POLITY OF THE METHODIST EPISCOPAL CHURCH WITH THE TEACHING OF THE SCRIPTURES, ON THE SUBJECT OF SLAVERY.

As we set out with the object of defending the present position and ecclesiastical law of the Methodist Episcopal Church from the charge of pro-slaveryism, and of showing its strict conformity to the teaching of the Holy Scriptures, in regard to this unhappy question, let us see, as far as possible, how closely they approximate.

To do this to the best advantage, it may be useful, at this stage of the investigation, to recapitulate the important principles elaborated from the Bible that bear directly on this question. And,

First. The Bible lays down the principle, that the incipient movement in this inhuman and Heaven-insulting business, is a crime of the greatest magnitude that a man can commit against his fellow-man, and deserving a corresponding punishment: "He that stealeth a man, and selleth him, or if he be found in his hand, shall surely be put to death."

The law of the Methodist Episcopal Church strikes at the root of this business, by declaring that none who buy men, women, (or) and children, with an intention to enslave them, can belong to her communion.

Second. When it has become an element of civil society, interwoven with all the relations of the social state, and hedged about with all the solemn forms and intricacies of law, in the hands of those who did not originate the evil, the Bible tolerates it, as compatible with the Christian character of both master and slave: "And they that have believing masters, let them not despise them, because they are brethren; but rather do them service, because they are faithful and beloved, partakers of the benefit. These things teach and exhort." 1 Tim. vi, 2.

The Methodist Episcopal Church, for the same reasons or considerations, allows it in her membership; as her law, declaring it a great evil, and requiring emancipation under circumstances specified in that law, abundantly proves. This is its spirit.

Third, The Bible, in tolerating it, throws all those guards around it which are calculated to make the very best of it under the circumstances.

The Methodist Episcopal Church, by her missions among slaves on the plantations, and her law requiring their religious instruction, and her members to allow them time for the public worship of God, does the same thing.

Fourth. The principles, spirit, and teaching of the Bible all conspire to declare it a great evil.

The laws of Methodism lift their voice in the same general condemnation: "We declare we are as much as ever convinced of the great evil of slavery."

Fifth. The Bible, as we have seen, manifestly looks to its final overthrow, by the power of Christian principle.

The laws of the Methodist Episcopal Church, that work the forfeiture of the ministerial character of those who are, or become connected with it, where the laws of the State will admit of emancipation, and allow the liberated slave to enjoy freedom, are, on this subject, "like the voice of one crying in the wilderness, Prepare ye the way of the Lord, make his paths straight."

Sixth. The Bible in its principles, spirit, and teaching, manifestly, and, as we think, rationally, supposes that the most wise, good, and holy men who embrace it, will occupy advanced ground, in furtherance of its achievements and moral triumphs, till all earth's jubilee shall be realized and proclaimed.

The laws and usages of Methodism, supposing her general superintendents, or bishops and preachers, to be the most wise and holy of the Church, endeavour to keep them as far as possible from the evil of slavery.

Seventh. The Bible seeks only by the power of moral goodness to subvert the principle, and thus break down the practice, without arraying the Church against the State.

The laws of the Methodist Episcopal Church recognize the supremacy of the civil power, as the ordinance of God. And only by the influence of the principles of moral goodness does she attempt to interfere in this matter. And as the great Master, who, by reason of the "weakness of the flesh," or hardness and unbelief of mankind, could not do all the good he would; so Methodism, in all her borders,* sighs over an evil beyond her power to remove.

Now how any man, with any semblance of truth, can deny her Scriptural position, and represent her as pro-slavery, is totally beyond our powers of con-

* At the time this was written, the author, judging from the language of the Discipline, and professions of sympathy for the condition of the poor slave which he had heard in behalf, and read from the pens of Southern Methodists, supposed he was giving utterance to nothing more than truth in this general declaration. Subsequent developments, or developments which have subsequently come to his notice, have led him in behalf of the South to doubt the correctness of the sentiment. Many of their distinguished men claim it to be Divinely appointed, and therefore right. Hence, there is, with those so understanding it, no occasion to "sigh over it."

ception. True, superficial minds, that scan the surface of things, without looking at it as connected with God's moral and providential government of the world, may see that slavery, in the language of Methodism, "is a great evil;" and from this mere glance at the surface, draw hasty and weak conclusions. But it is only this class that will do so. For, as we have before intimated, which is testimony of great weight in vindication of this last proposition, the Church has never presented a man, of acknowledged reputation as a critic or commentator, that supports the pretensions of these new measures.

We repeat, the laws of Methodism are so fully and entirely accordant with the Holy Scriptures on the subject of slavery, that we have sometimes been tempted to think that more than human wisdom presided in or over the deliberations which brought them to their present maturity, and conformed them so essentially to the pattern given in the "holy mount."

It is, however, claimed by some, and may be urged by others, that the laws of the Church which, under certain specified conditions, require the ministry to execute deeds of emancipation, should be of indiscriminate application to the whole Church. This objection appears to be of some weight; and as such, is entitled to attention.

There would seem to us to be two reasonable grounds in the premises, why the objection is not valid, and therefore has not the weight or importance attached to it. And,

First. According to the great law of Christianity, "It is required of a man according to what he hath, and not according to what he hath not." Now, from the very complicated manner in which the subject of this relation is presented in the Holy Scriptures, and the confusion of thought that has almost universally obtained among statesmen, ministers, and laymen, as to its comparative guilt or innocence, is it fairly to be presumed, that there is abroad in the Church and the world a sufficient amount of clear and discriminating light, to mark and determine the essential sinfulness of the simple relation to be such as to bar a creditable profession of religion in that relation? If the premises warrant the conclusion, such would be the duty, and such should be the law of the Church. But in view of the unsettled state of public and the Church's opinion, and that too among those who have had the best opportunities of arriving at definite and correct conclusions with regard to it, we dare not say, nor do we think any other sane mind will attempt to say, that such is the state of the question.

Secondly. The ministry is the property of the whole Church; and as such, in our peculiar economy, liable to removals from North to South, and from the South to the North, as may, in the wisdom of the Church, be judged best for the general good. And in this feature of Methodist polity, the Church, in view of the "weakness of the flesh," or present disordered state, in order the more effectually to carry out the great purposes of her mission, has adopted the great Christian law of expediency, as best suited to the providential circumstances of our existence; a principle that cannot so readily apply to the laity in their permanent locations.

In addition to the above, they, from their vocation as ministers, may rationally be supposed to be more conversant with the Scriptures, and therefore in the possession of more light on this subject, than belongs to the people generally; and hence, on the great law that "it is required according to what a man hath," discriminatingly responsible for a more elevated position. We therefore conclude, the objection is not well founded.

But it may be further urged, that this reasoning is too loose, on so grave a subject; that truth is truth, and duty is duty, arising from that truth; and that if truth is eternal, and slavery a violation of that truth, how can the standard of Christian duty, consistently with truth, be let down to the loose principles above stated? We reply, that while we admit, on the one hand, that truth is eternal, we claim, on the other hand, that it is also an eternal truth that the Divine administration cannot be carried on, on this or any other question of human responsibility, on any other principle than the one above laid down, that "it is required according to what a man hath, and not according to what he hath not." Now for the providential government of God to determine the bounds of our habitation, in connexion with this evil, and our whole education from infancy to manhood, such as to make the impression, if not of its rightfulness, at least of its comparative innocence; and if, in connexion with this, the revelation of God contains many tolerant allusions to it, which the most intelligent ultra-abolitionist never has and never can explain away, as not bearing on the relation; and, added to this, that the question is so mixed up in the teaching of the Scriptures with the other relative duties of society, that (to our knowledge, unless this should be so regarded) no man has as yet attempted to trace it in its connexion with the Divine administration, so as to dissipate the mists and darkness that hang around it, and show up clearly its true position;—we repeat, till this be done, and the question be made so clear and outstanding, as to be no longer one of "doubtful disputation," but unequivocally involving a principle of conscience, we cannot, on the great law above stated, be condemned in an administration of perfect rectitude. And if the principle holds good in the government of God, what sufficient reason have we for departing from it on the subject of this relation?

True Wesleyanism and kindred movements may, if they choose, return to the dark ages of popery, and revive the claim of Divine right to make void this principle of the law of God through their traditions, and thus set up that essentially tyrannical, proscriptive, and wicked principle, that denies the right of private judgment. But we humbly trust that the intelligence of the community is such as not to be gulled by these false appearances, however plausibly presented.

That the principle involved amounts to the grave charge we have brought against them, is clear from the following considerations:—

First. Our Maker has formed us with mental and moral powers, to seek and know the truth. And,

Secondly, Has given us a revelation containing the rules of moral duty suited to our capacities, and the circumstances of our existence; and has called upon us to "search the Scriptures," that we may know and do our duty.

Thirdly. Now if, in searching those Scriptures, after the best reasonings we can bestow upon the subject, aided by the best lights within our reach, we honestly arrive at the conclusion, that the simple relation which was found in existence at the time they were given is, while the relation providentially continues, by an act of providential government, tolerated as a measure of moral discipline, in civil, social, and religious society, and practice accordingly, what is to be done with us? Why, True Wesleyanism will not receive us to her altars, but unceremoniously hand us over to the devil, because we refuse to surrender the right of private judgment, and by consequence the right of conscience, to her holy care and keeping, and receive on this subject the law at her mouth.

And thus, in their zeal to liberate the bodies of two millions from the chains of civil bondage, they would enslave the minds of eighteen millions in the chains of intolerant bigotry—a bondage not only nine times worse, in point of numbers, but immeasurably worse with regard to principle. For slavery, with all its wrongs, allows, and to some extent labours and hopes for, the salvation of its subjects. But this fell principle damns you here, and both soul and body forever hereafter in hell. May we not rejoice that God is judge, and not these sectarian bigots!

In view of all that precedes, we think we are entitled to the following conclusions: That there are two classes of truths which bear upon the slavery relation.

First. The doctrine of essential right, or eternal rectitude, in the sense of unbending law, with which the principle of slavery cannot be reconciled. Now the laws of Methodism on the subject of slavery, which prohibit those who buy or sell men, women, and children, with an intention to enslave them, from a place in her communion, and declare slavery to be "a great evil," are the fair and true exponents of this first class of truths. For they proceed upon the principle that slavery is an essential moral wrong, and, as such, all who voluntarily connect themselves with, or aid and abet the system, are guilty of that wrong, and therefore cannot have a place in her communion.

Second. The second class of truths are, " That it is required according to what a man hath, and not according to what he hath not," &c., &c. Now this class of truths has respect to the providential circumstances of our existence,—circumstances in which we are unavoidably connected with evils we did not create, and cannot control, and which disqualify us for, or otherwise prevent our carrying out, the principles of essential right, or the original laws of nature.

Now the laws of Methodism, which allow and tolerate the Christian character of a man in the relation, when in the providential circumstances of his existence he is unavoidably connected with it, are the fair and true exponents of this last class of truths. And thus, so far as her position in this particular matter is concerned, she is essentially " the Church of the living God ; the pillar and ground of the truth,"—the support and defence of the truth of both covenants on this question. There is no getting away from this conclusion. You may as well undertake to unsettle the stabilities of the eternal throne.

PART FOURTH.

REFLECTIONS ON DIFFERENT SUBJECTS CONNECTED WITH THIS QUESTION.

SECTION I.

THOUGHTS ON TRUE WESLEYANISM.

Now if the doctrine of these pages be true, in agreement with the principles, spirit, and teaching of the Holy Scriptures, and confirmed by the voice of reason, in what light are we to regard those new measures, recently introduced and adopted by men professing a great zeal for the glory of God, as well as a burning love for their fellow-men, who organize Churches, making the relation, under all circumstances, a bar to Christian fellowship; can we, in the utmost stretch of charity, recognize them as being regularly in the order of scriptural, rational, and providential duty? We think not. Mark! the question is not, Have they not the right to do so? this may be granted; but the question is, Are they, in view of all the providential circumstances connected with the case, sustained by the authority of Scripture and the voice of reason, in such a movement? We repeat, for the reasons already assigned in these pages, we think not. True, we did once, in our haste, admit that "*even* True Wesleyanism *might* be a child of Providence," but on our sober second thoughts we beg leave thus publicly to take that back. That Providence may take True

Wesleyanism under its keeping, as it does other spurious and monstrous births, (it being the child of well-meant error,) and use it as far as possible for good, is not denied; for it is the special sphere and glory of Providence, to "bring good out of evil." Hence saith the apostle, "I will provoke you to jealousy by them that are no people, and by a foolish nation will I anger you." Rom. x, 19. So Providence may make use of the paucity and foolishness of True Wesleyanism, to provoke the world to think and act on this subject. Further, with our present light on this subject, we cannot admit. We are compelled, by the paramount authority of Scripture and reason, to set it down as an illegitimate offspring; or, to make the very best of it, all things considered will admit, an abortion,—come too soon; in which they differ from other sinners generally; they won't come when they are called. True Wesleyanism has come without being called, only so far as an uneasy, restless, factious disposition, instigated by a spirit of well-meant error, and it may be headed by his "honour" of Pandemonium, who through them would make havoc of the Church of God, by opening a hopeful door to the disaffected and aspiring in the ministry and laity, and drawing off a few weak-minded men, women, and children, with some of youthful ardent temperament, who cannot rationally be supposed to be well enough read in the Scriptures to understand this subject in all its phases and relations; and therefore, being imposed upon by superficial, specious first appearances, "leap before they look," or, in other words, act before they think. These together constitute their elements of success.

When we look at this subject in all its phases, that,

upon the whole, they ever have done any good, may be honestly doubted. That they have excited some feelings of pity for the poor slave, is freely admitted; but too generally it amounts to sympathy for those we have never seen, and hatred to those with whom we had lived without one jar of discord in the fellowship of the gospel, until a difference of opinion on this subject severed us. Now, if we have read and understood our Bible correctly, it is only necessary to multiply these achievements on a magnificent scale, to banish every vestige of pure religion from the earth, and leave it to the undisturbed possession of the prince of darkness.

But again. That some souls may have been converted, and believers strengthened and built up in the faith of the gospel, is not denied. And all this consistently with the principles of God's moral and providential government; He acknowledging and honouring his truth for its own sake, without regard to, or the approbation of, the instrumentality using it; as may be distinctly learned from the language of Christ: "Many will say unto me in that day, Lord, Lord, have we not prophesied in thy name? and in thy name cast out devils? and in thy name done many wonderful works? And then will I profess unto them, I never knew you; depart from me, ye that work iniquity." So that, on the principles here laid down by our blessed Lord, the fruit we may claim is not always conclusive of the correctness of our position. And moreover, it is at least possible, not to say likely, that the other organizations previously in the field would have done all this, and a great deal more, but for the manner in which public confidence has been confused and confounded, not to say in many instances entirely destroyed, by the bold and sleepless effort of unmeasured and exaggerated detraction, which the True Wesleyan body—ministry and laity generally—have been making since their organization.

And how far this may be an offset against what good they have done, or how far their evil in this respect may overbalance all their good, will only be known in the great day of our Lord Jesus Christ. Therefore, in view of the whole ground—when we reflect on the bonds severed, the confidence destroyed, the suspicions excited, the jealousies awakened, the loud contention kindled, the open strife enacted, the angry passions heated, the war of words repeated, and the loud laugh of infidelity, with the louder roaring, joyous laugh of hell, that has echoed through the ranks of those who, arm in arm, in open, sweet, and loving brotherhood, have taken the lead in this new movement—we conclude that they not only have done no good, but harm.

These, with the light we now have, are the deliberate convictions to which our observations and investigations of the subject have conducted us.

Now, in view of what precedes, we have a little friendly advice to give the True Wesleyans, and all others of kindred spirit; but we speak more particularly of them than others, from the consideration, that having been a Methodist from the days of our boyhood, we have paid some attention to her ecclesiastical platform on the subject of slavery, and consequently know more about the fallacy of their alleged grievances than we do of others; and withal we think many of them, both in the ministry and laity, to be well-meaning people, who are trying to live in the fear of God. On which account, heretofore, (though we honestly believe them in error,) in view of the weakness of the flesh, we have commingled with, and rendered them, in our very feeble manner, some little assistance in their religious movements. But to the advice: It is, unless they can overturn the doctrine of these pages, fairly and scripturally, and thereby prove themselves, in their present organization, to be, what we have denied, the child of Providence, to disband, and, doing honestly their first works over again, go back, in the spirit of humility and meekness, to the places from whence you came. This may be a hard task, especially after having ransacked the vocabulary of earth for degrading epithets, with which to reproach the mother that travailed, bore, and gave you suck; dandling you, in your spiritual infancy, on the knees of her tender, sleepless care; and, under Christ, her husband and head, has said a thousand times to your troubled heart, in a voice of soothing, cheering, comforting, and strengthening melody, "Come thou with us, and we will do thee good; for the Lord hath spoken good concerning Israel."

We repeat, the task may be a hard one; but the occasion demands it; even all that simple, artless honesty which follows truth and duty in the lowest vale of humiliation: and moreover, paradoxical as it may seem, like the Divine administration before alluded to, in going down, you go up; or, like the repenting, returning sinner, your abasement will be your exaltation. Or if you want a case still more apposite, we will give it to you in the example of the great Richard Watson, than which, no act of his eventful and useful life commands more fully the approval of all wise and good men. Like many of you, in the heat, folly, or indiscretion of youth, or the thoughtlessness of an unguarded hour, he expatriated himself from the Church of his early choice; but, followed with convictions of haste and impropriety in so doing, he humbly and unostentatiously returned.

We repeat the advice: disband and go back, unless you can prove yourselves to be a child of Providence. And this we think you cannot do, for reasons already in part assigned. For if our position be true with regard to this question, the Church that bore you is, by a figure of speech, the true "Jerusalem from above." This mother you have called a harlot, a brotherhood of thieves, the synagogue of Satan, and all that sort of dirty thing. "And as the serpent cast out of his mouth water as a flood after the woman, that he might cause her to be carried away of the flood," so you, to speak without a figure, have persecuted the Church of God.

The inference is clear. If the Methodist Episcopal Church, in her ecclesiastical polity, as we think we have established beyond controversy, is founded on the essential truth of God's word, He can never have raised you up for the purpose of defaming that Church, because, such is her position, this would be his "kingdom divided against itself."

SECTION II.

ON THE DIVISION OF THE CHURCH.

It may not be improper in us to offer some reflections on the division of the Church, as a matter we have greatly deplored, and over which, whenever our thoughts run in that direction, we yet mourn with sentiments of heartfelt sorrow; and often find ourselves, in our musings on this gloomy subject, overrun with the almost unconscious or involuntary wish, O that it had never come to pass! or, having come to pass, that the wisdom and goodness of all concerned, by the blessing of God, who is said to "bless his people with peace," might devise some ways and means by which the "hurt of the daughter of my people might be recovered." But, alas for poor Methodism! the battle increases—the breach widens; and the increasing developments that time and circumstances are evolving, give ominous signs that, in our intercourse, a cool, calculating, worldly policy is to swallow up (with profound emotion we name it) the gushing tide of warm, generous, glowing Christian affection that in the days of other years used to circulate throughout the whole heaven and earth of original Methodism. May He who presides in high and gracious authority over his militant care forbid it! and, if nothing better can be done,—of which we sometimes hope even against hope—hush the furious, raging, roaring storm that now agitates us, to—"In essentials, unity; non-essentials, liberty; and in all things, charity;"—that a fairer spring may bloom on our Zion, and drive away wintry storms forever.

On this subject doctors have differed; even doctors whose fame, religiously, has filled the measure of their country's glory. From which fact we are admonished of the feebleness, and fear the unavailingness of the effort of one who cannot affix to his signature the beautifully rounded period of D. D.; and is so peculiarly constituted, as not to like the prefix R-E-V. Nevertheless, with feelings of due deference to our predecessors, and possibly our superiors, on this subject, we will approach it, encouraged thereto, first, by the widow's mite, of renowned notoriety in sacred history; and, secondly, by what we find written in the Book of Job: "I said days should speak, and the multitude of years should teach wisdom. But there is a spirit in man, and the inspiration of the Almighty giveth understanding. Great men are not always wise; neither do the aged understand judgment. Therefore I said, Hearken unto me; I also will show mine opinion." In doing which, we shall endeavour, as far as possible, to avoid what has been already written, it now being before the public, and need not be here repeated.

A sentiment that some time since purposely escaped the pen of the catholic Hunter, of the Pittsburgh Christian Advocate, about a kindred matter, will, on this subject, be a good commencement. It was in reference to the family quarrel between Episcopal and Protestant Methodism, for which, with him, we see no gospel reason why they should longer be measuring their swords, and trying the weight of their metal. Like that, the division of the Church into North and South (however the North will not admit the cognomen) originated in a family quarrel, in which, we think, to a greater or less extent, both parties, as we will endeavour to show, are implicated; for we shall try to follow out our convictions of truth, giving saint and sinner their portion, cost our reputation what it may. But we forget, our memory being short in this matter, for on the other page we publish to the world we have none. Well, to commence over again: Have we of the North fully appreciated the difficulties of the South, and duly sympathized with them in their connexion with the great evil of slavery? We speak not of the laws which created and entailed it upon them, as claiming our sympathy; but of a state of things the present generation or Church did not create, and cannot control; and if they could, cannot, by reason of the complexity of the question, and the darkness that covers the Southern mind, see how to rid themselves of it, securing, at the same time, the good of all concerned. And, in this respect, we speak not of the light in which we, at our distance, may view it. It is too much like the man standing a distance off, and looking at another in some heavy lift; he thinks if he had hold of it he could manage it with apparent ease. Full of self-confidence, he steps forward, seizes hold, and after half a dozen ineffectual efforts, quietly walks off in his disappointment: so Yankee or Northern keenness cannot, at the distance of a thousand miles, see as far into this millstone as they who pick it. The subject, at best, has its difficulties, and most seriously so, in view of its legal and providential phases. The questions, How to remove it? and, What's to be done with it? are much more easily asked than answered.

Further, if in the providential government of God, without any fault of their own, they are, by inheritance, connected with it through the operation of laws they did not create, and cannot control, as we are fairly entitled to presume a great portion of the Southern Church is; and when we connect with this fact, their professions of sympathy for those whose condition they know not how to relieve, and that they regard slavery as a great evil; does not their situation rather claim our sympathy, than our hatred and vindictive denunciations? And are they not to be operated on as men of reason and humanity, by the principles and power of moral goodness, rather than by the coarse and maniac ebullitions of passion, which have marked the agitation of this question? Have we of the North been governed by these considerations? Have we studiously sought to conform our movements to this rule, which, in the principles and spirit of Christianity, is written on almost every page of Divine revelation? We speak not of the courtesy as a debt due to the South, which has been shown it in the deliberations of the General Conference, but of what has transpired without the court, in an individual and social capacity. To these interrogatories truth compels us to answer, that we think not. True, those who were the most active in this matter are not now of us; but they were in the commencement of the aggression. And however contrary to the general feelings and wishes of the Church, it had its tendency to goad and irritate the Southern feeling. And as "when wine is in, wit is out," is true of the laws of mind; so is it equally true, that a perturbed mind magnifies and enlarges real or supposed evils, until in its perverted vision, in matters both great and small, Alps rise on Alps, and finally the mountain load has crushed the unity of the Church. And as a worse result, if possible, the crash has opened fissures, not to say avalanches, that are sending forth their waters; not like those seen in the vision of the prophet, "coming down from under, from the right side of the house," and in their generous flow, healing everything that liveth or moveth, whithersoever they go; but bitter waters—waters of strife, contention, devastation, ruin, and death, which painfully and wofully, in a moral point of view, add to the miry places and marshes of a world which before had but too few green, flourishing, and fruitful spots.

But does all the sin in this matter lie at the door of the North? Verily we think not. "What we have written, we have written." And not one hair's breadth farther do we, according to our convictions of truth, feel at liberty to push the battle with our big gun, or, if you please, small-arms, against the North. And that too, keeping up the figure, with this reserve:—That our generals, and colonels, and captains, and corporals, and private soldiers, were, with few exceptions, opposed to this movement in its direction against the Church, it being confined principally to a few hot-heated, restless, and unruly in our ranks, together with deserters from us and others. And the magnanimous South, if they did not, might, and ought to have known this, and acted accordingly, which brings us, according to the plan we have marked out for ourself in this war of words and truth, to open our broadside, it may be of small-arms, upon the South. And as before intimated, we do not want, nor will we at present have much to do with those big guns, called, in common parlance on this subject, compromise laws, conventional articles, plans of division, &c. We will leave these for the big doctors, who cannot fight with anything but heavy metal; for we should only be trammelled with Saul's armour. It would not fit or suit us, no how. And after all the ado that is made about them, we do not think they have all come from the proper armoury—the gospel. We prefer our sling, with a few smooth stones from the brook of truth, which on this subject, as well as all others, is "profitable for doctrine, reproof, correction, and instruction in righteousness;" that we may be thoroughly furnished to every good word and work in this campaign of mental and moral conflict.

It will be remembered, that in these pages we have laid it down as a doctrine of the Bible, a principle of God's moral government, and as being sealed and authenticated by the spirit of Christianity, that slavery is a great evil, and only to be tolerated as a temporary regulation, in view of the weakness of the present disordered state of the world. Now the Methodist Episcopal Church has taken it into her communion just exactly in the shape in which it is presented in the Holy Scriptures. The likeness is perfect. No artist ever came nearer the original, as all who will read closely and attentively our ecclesiastical law, and compare it with the Scriptures, will be fully satisfied.

But again. Like as John, the forerunner of Jesus, was sent as a "voice crying in the wilderness, Prepare ye the way of the Lord, make his paths straight," so the Bible has sent out sentinels as the harbingers of this moral achievement, who have taken their stand "in the top of high places, in the way of the places of the paths, crying at the gates, at the entry of the city, at the coming in at the doors. Unto you, O men, I call, and my voice is to the sons of men. Hear, for I will speak of excellent things, and the opening of my lips shall be right things." And the cry is civilly to the nation or the state: "Is not this the fast that I have chosen? to loose the bands of wickedness, to undo the heavy burdens, and to let the oppressed go free, and that ye break every yoke?" and then, socially and individually, "all things whatsoever ye would that men should do to you, do ye even so to them." And again, "if thou mayest be made free, use it rather," and "be ye not the servants of men."

Now the likeness is here again perfect. Methodism has her sentinels out in advance of the present state of things on this subject,—in her law requiring her ministers connected with it, if practicable, to execute deeds of emancipation, and in refusing ordination to those in the relation who can emancipate, and the liberated slave enjoy freedom. And this is not a dead letter in the book of Discipline, to be read merely to keep up appearances. No! honour to the Baltimore Conference, which has always practised on this rule, and some additional honour to her talented Collins, for his noble defence, before the General Conference of 1844, of her Bible, Methodistic, and rational position on this subject.

"Now comes the tug of war." One of the sentinels that Methodism in good faith had placed on advanced ground, in the character of a good, wise, holy general superintendent or bishop, whose freedom from slavery as a Southern man, as we shall see in the sequel, constituted the controlling reason why he was chosen to that responsible office, and who, in that office, was expected to be a light in a dark place, somehow forgot his position, got astray, and with his eyes open to all the facts in the case, became entangled in the meshes of slavery. This matter comes with, or rather precedes him to the General Conference, the tribunal of his responsibility. Inquiries with regard to the truth of Madam Rumour's report are instituted, when, lo and behold! to the consternation and overwhelming grief of the great body of the Church, it was found to be true on his own acknowledgment. True, he tried to patch it, but made it the worse for patching. For the best tailor we have ever seen could not, taking ever so much pains, and stitching ever so nice, sew a few jet black patches on a pure, fine, white, flowing robe, without making it look the worse. He might get all the bishops, and all the presiding elders, and all the preachers, and all the lawyers, and all the doctors too, if he pleased, to help him, and all would not avail; the people would see its beauty marred, its purity stained, its glory departed.

Now, after all that has been said, written, and published on this subject, some of it possibly to divert attention, becloud our vision, and palliate and justify this measure, this is the exact, true, and unvarnished state of the question. And what is to be done? Must the whole Church, east, west, north, and south —ay, the whole heaven and earth of Methodism, face to the music of this retrograde movement, and thus dim the lustre of her Scriptural and exceeding glory, as compared with some of the sister Churches on this subject; and by so doing, give up one of her Bible marks, as a child of Providence, raised up to spread Scriptural holiness over these and all other lands? God forbid! And I liked to have said, it would have been better for her to have given up the ghost in the womb of Providence, than thus ignobly to have surrendered the mark of the Man of Calvary for the mark of a beast, and a black beast at that. No, never. As the venerable Griffith said on a kindred subject, "Stand alone in your glory first." This principle of Methodist polity is to the coming glory of the Church, what the star of the East was to the coming Messiah. And shall we suffer, or help to draw a black cloud over it? No! not as the sons of the immortal Wesley, or, more nobly still, the sons of God. The question to cursory observers may be regarded of small moment; and we are inclined to the opinion, that such is the light in which it falls on the mind's eye of the South. But the converse of a former proposition, in allusion to their difficulties on this perplexed question, is, in this phase of the subject, true. That is, persons at a distance, and unconnected with it, can see its moral bearings to better advantage than those whose connexion and familiarity, from infancy to manhood, with its wrongs, have dimmed the lustre of their mental and moral vision. Just as a man from a low, damp, swampy, smoky, foggy position, cannot have the same clear and distinct view of a distant object, as another with equal organs of vision can, from a more elevated or commanding position; or, according to the laws of sight, some objects may be too near us for clear and distinct vision. Perhaps the thought would be better expressed, by saying the object is in too close contact with the Southern eye, for that nice discrimination of which the magnanimous South would be fully capable, under a change of circumstances. This, by many, may be regarded as too great a concession. But the voice of reason, aside from the dictates of Christian charity, requires us to give the best construction that the nature of the case will allow. But, after all, we regard the subject in a very different point of light. As involving principle, and principle of the most elevated character, to say the very least of it we dare, it is, in essence, a scintillation of that moral goodness which devised, executed, and consummated the redemption of the world by Jesus Christ; and by which our spiritual, and the poor slave's civil chains, if ever it be done by earth or heaven, are to be broken off, which may Heaven grant for that goodness' sake. We believe the South to be wrong on this subject; but, we still hope, magnanimously wrong, and will leave it for time and circumstances to determine.

Before we close our reflections on this subject we have a word to say about it, in the light of the so-called compromise laws. We think we did not entirely interdict ourself in our former playful remarks about them. In reference to the design of these laws, there seems to be a difference of opinion between the North and the South; the North claiming them as a matter of accommodation to the peculiar circumstances of their southern brethren, and the South claiming that they form, and were intended for, a compromise law, on which, as a common platform, they stand side by side with their brethren of the North, guaranteed and protected in all their privileges, even to a slaveholding bishop. Having thus honestly, and, as we think, fairly, on this subject, stated the distinctive and respective ground occupied by the North and South, we have done with it for the present. Which side has truth and right in this controversy is not now under consideration. And whatever bearing this phase of the question would be entitled to in a case fairly coming up under, or covered by these laws, is another and a very different question from the one now before us; which is, Was the Rev. James O. Andrew elected to the general superintendency of the Methodist Episcopal Church, with the distinct understanding, on the part of both North and South, that it was under the compromise laws as interpreted by the South. If this can be fairly and unequivocally made out, the South, in view of the action of the General Conference in his case, had just grounds of complaint, and, so far as ecclesiastical law is concerned, greatly grieved and maltreated in the person of their Bishop. But are these the facts in the case? or rather, is not the very reverse true? Was he not elected with the distinct understanding, known to himself, the South, and the North, that he was a southern man, unconnected with slavery? Just exactly on the principles of the North, the principles and usages of Methodism, and the principles of the Bible, as contended for in these pages; which is, that the most wise, holy, and good men—which bishops are, or should be—will occupy advanced ground on this and all kindred subjects. The reported debates of the General Conference prove all we here assume. On page 148 the Bishop admits that brother Winans (a southern man) told himself, J. O. Andrew, at the General Conference of his election, that he could not vote for him, because he (brother Winans) believed that he (James O. Andrew) was nominated for the episcopacy because he was not a slaveholder. It is also established beyond all controversy, from the face of the same document, that the amiable and talented Capers suggested him for the office, because he was a southern man, unconnected with slavery. Whatever, at the time, may have been the doctor's unexplained opinions of Southern rights, secured, as they claim, by those compromise laws, and we don't mean to insinuate the most remotely that the doctor acted the part of duplicity in this matter, it is irrefragably true, that the nomination did not proceed in open court, in recognition of those rights. The doctor was desired, if possible, to free himself from the relation, that he might be chosen to that office. His reply, according to the testimony of brother Davis, of the Baltimore Conference, and to which the doctor, though present, and immediately concerned in the matter, by way of explanation, took no exceptions, was "that himself (Doctor Capers) was a slaveholder, and doomed to remain a slaveholder, and in this alternative that the doctor did nominate James O. Andrew to the caucus committee, would not be denied, because it could be proved by more than a dozen there."—*Conference Debates,* page 99. And on page 142 of the same document it will be found that Doctor Smith, of Virginia, admits that he had some knowledge of this matter, viz.: That James O. Andrew was nominated because he was a southern man, unconnected with slavery; and that for this reason, and this reason alone, he did not vote for his election.

We will pause here a moment, to ask the reader a question. Is it very probable, or can we suppose it even possible, that these four southern brethren, viz., James O. Andrew, Doctors Winans, Capers, and Smith, together with brother Davis, and the more than a dozen of whom he (Davis) speaks in his testimony, were all that had any knowledge that the nomination of James O. Andrew to the general superintendency of the Methodist E. Church was because he was a southern man unconnected with slavery, and a profound secret to all the other members of the General Conference present? We repeat, is there the most distant probability that this question was locked up exclusively in the breasts of these men? Impossible. The character and tendency of the case to excite feelings of interest; the jealousies that were rife (as leaks out in the testimony of southern members) between the different sections of the country on this subject, and the known laws of human nature to be excited, and to communicate the cause, and give expression to such excitement, absolutely forbid the conclusion. Now, in view of the above facts,—unmistakable facts; facts that are outstanding to the world, as matters of documentary record, and which therefore may be known and read of all men, and which, too, are a triumphant refutation of the argument of Doctor Smith, on page 141, where he charges the North with having deceived the South, in the election of James O. Andrew to the general superintendency; we repeat, in view of the above facts,—facts that are sustained at the bar of public opinion, or before an intelligent universe, if you please, by the testimony of southern members, they "standing alone in their glory," as may be seen by reference to the pages of the document here quoted; is it not as clear as that two and two make four, that the election of James O. Andrew to the general superintendency of the M. E. Church, proceeded upon the conceded and well-authenticated fact, to both North and South, that he was a southern man unconnected with slavery? No matter of historic record can be more clear and indubitable. And why now, with a confidence that is rebuked, and should stand abashed and confounded in the presence of these facts, bring up a law of, at least, controverted and doubtful authority, and apply it to this principle of Methodistic usage, to cover, protect, and defend this case? We will not charge the magnanimous South with low intrigue, or overt management in this matter; but we are compelled, from the commanding evidence before us, to believe that they have made a false issue, or have attempted to shield it by a law of doubtful authority, at best, which has not, and in all fairness cannot have, even a shadow of application to the case. And such, we think, when the whole question is fully and fairly understood, will be the verdict of intelligent public opinion.

According to current report, Bishop Andrew felt his difficulties, and came to the General Conference with the design of resigning his office, but was resisted and dissuaded from that purpose by the southern delegation. This fact, however manifestly and outstandingly insufficient, in the presence of the facts above stated, to screen, cover, or protect him from the charge of moral delinquency, will, to some extent, mitigate the severity of public judgment. But after all he is in the wrong, and the pages of impartial history will so record it.

There is yet another light in which we may take a glance at this painful subject. It was alluded to by the venerable Bangs, on the floor of the General Conference; and is unquestionably, from the whole character of Christianity, not only of Christian obligation, but of great practical utility. We mean the law of expediency, as laid down by the apostle in the following language: "If meat make my brother to offend, I will eat no flesh while the world standeth, lest I make my brother to offend."

Now the principle here stated commends itself to our understanding, as the offspring of a magnanimous mind, and generous heart; and as such, by the force of its own intrinsic excellence, commands our admiration. But when viewed in the light of the Divine administration, which is an expedient of boundless goodness, to make the best of circumstances, for the salvation of a sin-disordered world, it receives additional strength, and appeals to us in all that weight of moral goodness which characterized the magnanimous Redeemer, in condescending, not to what we had a right to claim, according to the eternal principles of rectitude, the laws of nature, or the social rights of man, as growing out of those principles, but to weakness, shame, and pain, that He thereby might accomplish our world's redemption; and in so doing has left us an example that we should follow his steps. Now who is it that cannot see that Bishop Andrew has offended against this rule? He knew, according to his own statement, that his southern brethren regarded his election as proceeding on the fact that he was not a slaveholder; and also the acute feeling of the great body of the Church on that subject. And however he might feel disposed to disregard clearly implied faith to both North and South, by claiming that he was not personally approached and his views elicited on that subject, and then throwing himself back on the compromise laws as interpreted by the South, and thus make good his right to do as he did; he, as a Christian bishop, was still bound by this law of expediency to regard in this matter the feelings of his brother, and much more the feelings of the great body of the Church.

But it is objected that the Northern feeling on this subject is too fastidious, and therefore not to be regarded. Not more so, no, not so much so as the feeling of the South. For, according to the Scriptures, God has appointed meat to be in part the food of man; but, as we have seen, has never appointed slavery; and only tolerates it in view of the "weakness of the flesh," under the controlling power of circumstances. Would not our Southern brethren do well to look at the subject a little in this direction? It would, as we hope, operate to destroy the delicacy and squeamishness of Southern feeling; not only by the goodness of the principle involved, but by all the force of the difference between positive Divine appointment on the one hand, and bare toleration on the other.

And we must contend, that a due regard for this law of expediency, apart from the gross and palpable wrongs of the system of American slavery, will sustain the ecclesiastical law and usage of Methodism, in requiring her ministry, when practicable, to emancipate their slaves, or otherwise forfeit their ministerial character; and in keeping her general superintendency free from it, lest thereby that superintendency becomes embarrassed and disqualified for its special and appropriate work. The world then knows that Methodism, not only in word, regards "slavery as a great evil," but in deed;—and like the Redeemer, and the Bible, only consents, under the circumstances, to tolerate it. Whereas the position, as contended for by the South, on this subject, and on which they have sacrificed the unity of Methodism, and to which they have subsequently conformed their practice, by electing two additional slaveholding superintendents, is a complete nullification of our ecclesiastical law, rendering it a dead letter, and which, for consistency's sake, should have some black marks drawn around them, or be expunged from the Book of Discipline. For, in the language of Dr. Elliott, who always says something when he speaks or writes: "If the three most holy men of the South [such bishops should be] are extensively connected with it, [with a fourth one for their apologist,] it becomes a holy thing." Or, at least, not so bad, but that all who can, both saint and sinner, may safely follow such holy examples, set them in the character and practice of the Southern bishops, and justified by the Southern Church.

These may be regarded as rather caustic remarks. If our position on this subject be correct, not more so than its nature and importance demand. And while we have endeavoured, for the sake of the truth, to call things by their right names, we are deeply conscious of not having used one word or sentence for the purpose of offence.

Now, if the facts in reference to the election of James O. Andrew to the general superintendency of the Methodist Episcopal Church, be as we have stated, and from the debates of the General Conference have proved them to be,—the South themselves being the witnesses summoned to the bar, and deposing to their verity,—and if the principles of the Bible be as we have stated,—and we confidently challenge controversy on either aspect of the question,—we repeat, if the grounds we occupy in these pages be correct—the violation of which, on the part of the South, has led to the overthrow of the unity of Methodism—if they cannot, by Scripture, by reason, and by an exhibition of counter facts, of equal or more notorious verity, set them aside; what is their duty as a body of Christians, and Christian ministers? Why, if the division of the Church, and the private and public criminations and recriminations along the borders, and everywhere else, have done no more, which is far from being the whole truth in the case, than to violate the inspired injunction, "Let brotherly love continue"—it is plainly and obviously their duty to retract the offensive step; and, by thus repairing their own wrongs, restore, as far as may be, the wonted feeling of Christian affection and brotherhood, that used to circulate throughout our entire Zion. Nothing short of this, in a gospel sense, will meet the emergency. Every species of real or expedient evasion, under whatever pretexts it may be attempted to be introduced or practised, is inadmissible. Our holy Christianity requires "truth in the inward parts,"—the truth, the whole truth, and nothing but the truth; and that from the heart. And it requires it from organizations, whether political, social, or religious, as well as from individuals.

The rule is of nice discrimination and application,—"searching the heart and trying the reins;" and, in default thereof, there is no way to have a good conscience,—mark! a good conscience,—one fully illuminated and regulated by the principles, spirit, and power of Christianity, either as individuals, or collective bodies, but by retracting our wrong, if possible; and, if not practicable, by openly confessing that wrong. This, we acknowledge, in view of position, the pride of opinion, and surrounding circumstances, is a difficult task; especially among men of great reputed wisdom, whom everybody supposes to know everything. Nevertheless, if truth from the hidden secrets of the heart, and a good conscience, require it, we should lay our honour in the dust, magnanimously confessing and forsaking our error. It matters not how high we are; the greater the stoop, the greater the elevation. For a remark before made is true in this matter, in going down, we go up; and, in the language of Solomon, "Before honour is humility."

But enough, and, some may think, by far too much of this homily, especially from one whom nobody knows, and nobody scarcely ever heard tell of, save a few of his friends, and neighbours, and acquaintances; and among whom, like other prophets, he is without honour; and who would feel it an honour, and a zest of enjoyment, to sit at the feet of many of these brethren, and learn from them the lessons of wisdom and salvation.

But in the event our Southern brethren cannot, on the questions herein involved, fairly silence the truthful roar of our small-arms, what will they do? Will they, like the prodigal of the gospel, come back, in the spirit and language of honest and hearty confession? We, for one, will promise them, that the mother, if not the father, (of which there is no doubt,) will meet them on that return, with all the tenderness of maternal affection.

But a voice from the General Conference at Pittsburg whispers in our ear, in behalf of the South, We did come! But how did you come? Ah, there's the rub! Why, like the Pharisee of the gospel, in the language of justification, instead of humiliation. One thought more, and we have done. Heaven never struck terms with the most honourable sinner, or, may be more appropriately, with the most honourable backslider, on such conditions.

SECTION III.

ON THE CONDITION OF AFRICA—AFRICAN SLAVERY AN ACT OF PROVIDENTIAL GOVERNMENT.

THE moral and providential government of God, although very much blended in the divine administration over the world, are separate and distinct acts of governing power; which is a discrimination of great importance in this investigation. For an act or measure that could not, on principles of simple, rigid law, be tolerated, without impeaching the character and government of God, may, in the Divine administration, as a principle of providential government, with great propriety be taken hold of and tolerated, for the sake of its practical utility; and the more especially so, when all the circumstances of the case clearly vindicate the Divine administration from having been accessory to the original act, or first introduction of such measure.

The case of Joseph and his brethren is apposite, and luminously illustrative of the subject now under consideration. Now, apart from the providential phases of this transaction, their conduct in their enmity to, and the sale of, Joseph, their brother, into Egypt, could not have been tolerated; for, as it appears to us, it would have been a great stain, not to say a great reproach, to the Divine administration, to have supposed that the moral Governor of the world should lend his toleration to such conduct; and yet we are distinctly informed in the Holy Scriptures that such is the fact: "And he said, I am Joseph your brother, whom ye sold into Egypt. Now therefore be not grieved nor angry with yourselves that ye sold me hither; for God did send me before you to preserve life." Gen. xlv, 4, 5. From which, with what follows in the succeeding verses, it is clear that the Divine toleration was extended to the transaction; not in the sense, however, that justified their conduct, and rendered them guiltless in the hatred and sale of their brother,—which, understood in a strictly moral point of view, would have been an impeachment of the Divine administration,—but as a providential act of government, by which their evil designs and doings might be overruled for the accomplishment of great, visible, and lasting good, which was the design, and which was the result, as the sequel clearly and abundantly proves; for not only the Egyptians and the family of Jacob were preserved thereby, but other nations also, "for the famine waxed sore in all lands."

Now when we look at the whole transaction in this light, whatever may be the demerit attaching to the conduct of the brethren of Joseph, as an act of providential government, the blended wisdom and goodness of Providence shine forth in such rays of exceeding glory, as to command our adoring homage, rather than to excite any dissatisfaction on account of the apparent diffiulties connected with it.

And another feature in the providential history of this case which claims our attention is, that although Joseph, and finally the family of Jacob, were in humbled circumstances while in Egypt, the land of their providential oppression, all things considered, it was the best for them, and the best for the world, that they did for a season sojourn in that land. The matter is so clear in the individual case of Joseph, whom "God made lord over all Egypt," that there is no difficulty in regard to him; and to a moment's candid reflection the case, if not exactly in the same sense, must, we think, be equally apparent in reference to the family of Jacob, which, as stated in the Scriptural narrative, was doubtless preserved in existence by this act of Providence. And so with regard to Egypt, and all other countries,—"for the famine waxed sore in all lands."

Another beneficial result very obvious from this act of providential government, and doubtless of vast importance to the Egyptians, and through them to the world, was a diffusion of the knowledge of the true God,—the mighty God of Abraham, Isaac, and Jacob,—as being superior to all the gods of Egypt, and the gods of all other lands; which was made known and vindicated, not only in the history of Joseph, but in the signs and wonders wrought by the hand of Moses before the court of Pharaoh, and in the outstretched arm of Jehovah in the various outstanding miracles that marked their return to the land of Canaan. Who can look at all this sum of good to the race, as the result of this providential government, and feel in his heart any other emotion than that of the most profound gratitude and admiration at the depth and overflowing goodness of His counsels?

Now, as above intimated, and as it appears to us, this act of providential government will apply to and illustrate, in some of its aspects, African slavery.

The teaching of the Holy Scriptures, and the history of the Divine administration, abundantly prove that individuals, churches, and nations may, by a course of obstinate and persevering neglect, or abandoned iniquity, forfeit the privileges of their probationary existence. Frequent allusions are made to such a state of things in the sacred writings. In the book of Revelation churches are threatened with the removal of their candlesticks. The lovely Jesus, in approaching the city of Jerusalem, said, "O that thou hadst known, even thou, in this thy day, the things that belong to thy peace; but now they are hid from thine eyes." And Paul, when addressing the Jews, said, "Seeing that ye count yourselves unworthy of eternal life, lo we turn to the Gentiles." Other instances might be multiplied, did we deem it necessary; but these we think are sufficient.

Now from our reading, which, were it more general, would warrant a more matured opinion, it has occurred to us, that this, in a providential point of light, is the condition of Africa.

That they had the tidings of salvation on the first announcement of the Gospel, we learn from the Acts of the Apostles; in which it is stated, that, on the memorable day of Pentecost, there were present devout men from every nation under heaven; who were all witnesses of the wonderful works of God.

Either too deeply sunk in mental and moral imbecility to be capable of it, or failing to improve the offer of salvation then made, and, as a natural result, sinking more deeply into mental and moral darkness and pollution, they appear finally to have been so lost to all sense of mental and moral culture, as to have become incapable, on their own soil, of a national experiment for their recovery from the deep state of darkness and moral imbecility into which, as a nation, they had fallen.

This may be regarded as a gloomy thought, and as visionary as any other hallucination of the wildest imagination. But such is the conclusion to which our reflections on this complex subject have conducted us; and which, we think, is not wholly without a parallel in the history of the Divine administration.

Those instances of a providential government which we have recorded in the Scriptures,—as the destruction of the world, on account of its wickedness, by a flood of waters, save Noah and his family; that which confounded the language of the world at the tower of Babel; that which destroyed the cities of Sodom and Gomorrah by fire from heaven; that which first selected a single family, and then a single nation, to be the depositories of the true religion; and that which finally sent the family of Jacob, as we have just seen, into a foreign oppression in the land of Egypt; and all these as judicial and gracious experiments of a providential government, for the instruction of mankind in the deep evil of sin, and the reformation of the world in righteousness,—are of a kindred nature with the theory of Providence we have suggested in reference to the African race.

Now on the supposition that our conjecture, in reference to the condition of Africa, be true, how is that condition to be reached? A repetition of the former experiments to which we have alluded, seems not to be the order of the Divine government; and, apart from this consideration, whatever amount of good they really did in the first instance accomplish, as an effectual and universal remedy, they appear to have failed; and their repetition, therefore, in all probability, would not have terminated in more satisfactory results.

The extremity and necessity of their condition required assistance. And what is to be done? The ordinary methods of Providence had failed; and there

9*

would seem to be no alternative but a resort to some extraordinary measure; and what measure can the utmost grasp of mind conceive, apart from the one here indicated, that does not absolutely involve the return of the age of miracles, for the expectation of which we have no warrant from the Scriptures.

It may be objected here, that this view involves most serious difficulties. Granted. But the case to be managed is one of equally obvious and outstanding difficulty; and extreme cases require extreme measures, and always justify them, when the good realized as a whole is more than equal to the injury inflicted. And that such is the case in this providential measure, we think is susceptible of proof; and that, too, apart from the instruction it may afford not only our world, but all other worlds, on the exceedingly unnatural and deeply evil character of sin, as will be seen in the sequel, and which must be a lesson of vast importance to all intelligent, free, and accountable beings. We claim, then, that the assistance their condition required was providentially granted, in their enslavement by and among those nations of the earth in which civilization and Christianity had obtained, and which nations, like Joseph's brethren, were wicked enough to engage in this nefarious business. And as the result, by their contact with civilization and Christianity, they will be elevated, in the lapse of time, from the depths of their ignorance and moral degradation, to such an acquaintance with letters and religion, as shall qualify them to return to their native country as the heralds of Christianity and civilization; and, by this process of providential government, pour that flood of light and salvation on benighted and degraded Africa, which shall elevate, renovate, and reinstate her to her proper rank among the nations and kingdoms of the earth.

And what a glorious consummation of Divine Providence, that Africa is to be redeemed, regenerated, and saved, by the instrumentality of her own returned children, who, themselves, were prepared and fitted for this work by the workings of an inscrutable, though benignant Providence, in the illuminating, refining, and elevating fires of a foreign bondage!

This, as we look at it, seems to be the order of Providence; our wickedness in their oppression having providentially cut us off from the privilege and glory of the accomplishment of this vast sum of good to Africa, as the active agents on that field of labour.

In the retributive justice of Providence, it will be ours to bear the burdens, and theirs to reap the glory, of this wondrous achievement of goodness and of grace.

Should their mental and moral condition as a nation be as we have conjectured; and should they finally, as the result of a partial bondage for a short season in this country, be lifted up as a nation from the great depths of their fall, this view of the subject will be a sufficient vindication of the goodness of that providential act of government, that suffered, for a time, their partial oppression in a foreign land, in view of their final elevation at home.

But if, in connexion with this, under that yoke of foreign oppression, their condition, as a whole, in reference to both time and eternity, is better than their condition in their own country, the goodness of Providence will, in this matter also, be incontrovertibly established, and the ways of God fully justified. And that such, with all the disadvantages of their present condition, is the fact, so far as letters, civilization, and religion are concerned, is, if the sources of our information be correct, undeniable. All of which conspire to assure us of the immeasurable depths of the ignorance and depravity into which they, as a nation, have fallen. Our views in this comparative estimate of condition in Africa or America are not restricted to the body, but include the soul; and no conceivable amount of bodily suffering can weigh against its present and eternal interests.

And in reference to the present world, bad as their condition is admitted to be here, it is fairly to be presumed that, as a whole, it is as good, if not really better, than in their own country. That there may be exceptions to the rule is not denied. But this is not the principle by which to determine this question. If, as a whole, or, in other words, if any considerable proportion of them are, or have it in their power, by proper personal effort, to be in better circumstances in their foreign oppression, than in their native land; this, we think, is, to all reasonable men, a sufficient proof of the goodness of Providence. Narrow minds may think differently, but none but narrow minds will so think. And that there is quite a proportion of them in improved circumstances, as the result of their present condition, may be fairly inferred from the following considerations:

First. That about one-third of the whole amount of our coloured population are freedmen; and are, or might be, in a much better condition than in benighted Africa.

In the second place; allowing that which has not even the probability of truth for its support; that one-half of the remainder are in a worse condition in this, than they were in their own country, it gives the result of two to one,—or two-thirds of the whole coloured population of this country, as being improved in their condition, so far as it concerns the present life, as compared with their condition in Africa.

Our means of information on this subject may not be such as to enable us to pronounce with absolute certainty on the correctness of all the conjectures here suggested. Nevertheless, we believe them to be true. And if such be the fact, how luminously glorious does the wisdom, goodness, justice, and holiness of Providence, in this wonderful arrangement, appear.

As above intimated, this general view of this question is not designed to extenuate or justify our wickedness in their oppression; but simply to show the vigilance of Providence, in making use of the wickedness of mankind in carrying out the purposes of his goodness toward benighted Africa.

SECTION IV.

ON THE DUTY OF THE GOVERNMENT.

If, as we have seen, the Scriptures regard slavery as a great evil, tolerating it, as an element of organized society, only in view of the "weakness of the flesh," or the disordered state of the world; and if, by the same high and paramount authority, the Church, under the existing circumstances, is in this matter, in the sense explained, and to the extent stated in the preceding pages, subordinate to the State; and in her organized capacity, with due regard to Scriptural precedent, cannot move in advance of the action of the State, what is the duty of the government in the premises? The fact, that the Divine administration, in mercy to our weakness, has taken hold of it as an element of society, making the best of it that infinite wisdom and goodness can, under the circumstances, never was intended,—nor can it be pleaded in our justification as a state or nation, in the continuance of this oppression; especially, if it may be fairly presumed that, as a state or nation, we have that amount of light and information, on the principles of God's moral and providential government of the world, which will enable us to understand its true position, and the reasons of its toleration. And until we are fairly entitled to the conclusion, that such is the amount of public intelligence on this subject, it is not rational to suppose that our responsibilities as a nation are so great as they otherwise would be. For it is only required of nations, as of individuals, "according to what they have, and not according to what they have not." And that it is to be presumed that this nation, as a nation, has the necessary amount of light on this subject, to form a correct public conscience, is to our mind a matter of very serious doubt. And that for the following reason: That the Christian ministry, whose only business it is to study and understand this, with other subjects connected with the Divine administration, are themselves greatly divided in their sentiments on this subject, occupying the extremes of the poles in relation to it. Some of them contend openly, others believe privately, that the Scriptures authorize the conclusion, that it is a Divinely appointed institution. Others, that there is nothing to be found in all the Scriptures that will warrant the shadow of such a conclusion, but entirely the reverse; and that, when properly understood, there is not the most distant tolerant recognition of the practice. While another class, which, in all probability, is far the most numerous, are all confusion in their reflections on the subject, and therefore have come to no settled conclusions whatever. They see and feel it to be an evil, but how to pronounce upon it, as a whole, they know not. Now, if those whose opportunities are the most favourable to a correct understanding of this subject, and whose business, as a part of their sacred calling, is to investigate and elaborate it, are thus divided and unsettled in the views which they, with equal confidence, profess to derive from the Holy Scriptures; by what principle of sound reasoning are we entitled to the conclusion, that the masses, or even our most prominent active politicians, are so well informed as to have and give a correct public conscience in reference to this question? We believe there is none. And therefore the impropriety of those severe anathemas, from the pulpit and the press, unaccompanied with, or preceded by, those discriminating, clear, and luminous instructions, that rationally and unequivocally give the rule of duty, on the high and unerring authority of "Thus saith the Lord." Till this be done, all such denunciations are perfectly gratuitous;—and, to make the very best of them, they are the offspring of a zeal not according to knowledge, for the plain and obvious reason involved in the apostle's argument, that "where there is no law there is no transgression." It is not intended to be intimated that we have not, in the Holy Scriptures, a law on this subject. The contrary we believe to be the fact. But, from the manner in which the question is mixed up with the moral and providential government of God, as taught in the Holy Scriptures, erroneous, confused, and unsettled notions have obtained; the rule of duty is not clear and distinct; and therefore liable to the same extenuation that would apply to individuals, who, under like difficulties, would be slow to arrive at correct conclusions with regard to the rule of individual duty in other matters.

Now if this reasoning is, as we suppose it to be, correct, it is clear that there must be more unanimity in the views of the Church or ministry, as the guides of public sentiment in this branch of public morals. In vain may it be urged as contrary to the law of nature and the dictates of conscience, as determined by that rule, while there is a lurking sentiment abroad that a higher authority has authorized it. And equally ineffectual will that course be, which denies in toto that the instructions of the Scriptures have any reference to a state of slavery. The contrary doctrine is too outstandingly obvious on the plain face of the sacred text, for men of reflection and discernment to be gulled into that opinion, by all the ignorant and vehement denunciation that may be brought to bear upon the question; so that it appears to us that an entire change, as to the manner in which this investigation is conducted, is imperiously demanded, as preparatory to intelligent and well-concerted political action.

Let the subject, in the exercise of calm and dispassionate reason, with due deference to the weakness of the present state, be thoroughly examined in the light of the Holy Scriptures, in its connexion with the principles and spirit of Christianity, and the government of God. And surely if the Bible teaches anything very clear and distinct on this subject, we may arrive at some unanimity of sentiment, to serve as a common ground on which to concentrate public opinion.

We repeat, till this be done, we may not rationally expect an intelligent public sentiment to give clearly the rule of public duty, and a correct public conscience to carry out that rule, any more than we can rationally expect an effect, either in morals or in physics, without an adequate cause.

When this shall have been accomplished, or when the subject shall have been disabused from the contradiction, darkness, and confusion, which have, and still mark the history of its investigation, and is placed in a clear, distinct, and unsophisticated light before the people, it will commend itself to their intelligence with all the power of truth; a correct public conscience will be created, and the way scripturally and rationally prepared for such action as the exigencies of the case shall demand.

For it is not to be concealed, if we would meet the question candidly and fairly, that after all this shall have been accomplished, there still remain difficulties of a serious nature to be examined and overcome. We would not be thought, nor do we fear that the intelligent will regard us as unnecessarily multiplying difficulties, by the enumeration of those which, in truth and soberness, belong to the question. And we should not, and will not, be deterred from the expression of our honest convictions of truth and duty, by the clamours of ignorance, recklessness, and fanaticism.

That it is the duty of our national and State Governments to do all in their power to repair their own wrongs to injured Africa, has already been stated as the doctrine of these pages; but how far they are bound, on the principles of ethical, political, or moral justice, to repair the wrongs of a previously existing and distinct government, which is a principle involved in this question, we are not competent to decide; and will therefore content ourselves with throwing out the suggestion, that, if it has not been already done, some competent pen may undertake it, and bless the world with its thorough examination.

This, as above intimated, is the shape of this question, as connected with the civil and social regulations of this country. The government of Great Britain, we believe, when this country was known as the British Colonies of North America, first introduced or suffered its introduction here; which fact, as we think, is to be received in mitigation of our demerit, or dereliction of duty. True, after our independence was declared, and our national existence acknowledged, we have followed in this matter the example set us by the former government; and by so doing have set the seal of our approval to its wrongs. But so true is it of all wrong, and "that evil communications corrupt good manners," that but for that example it might never have been introduced into this country. For it is fairly to be presumed, from the prevailing sense of liberty and equal rights that seems to have been prevalent at the time of the organization of this government, that had it not been previously introduced among us as an element of the civil and social state, it could not have been introduced. It appears to us that it is only necessary for us to be conversant with the general sentiment of the times, and particularly the sentiments on this subject of many of the master and leading spirits of the day, to be fairly conducted to this conclusion. For it is a matter of public record, and outstanding notoriety, that it well-nigh operated to defeat the glowing enthusiasm of our patriotic forefathers in the organization of this federal republic. And we think, after a somewhat careful and candid examination of the subject, it was only consented to, at least, in some of its phases, lest a contrary course might, directly or indirectly, endanger the great experiment of human liberty, or free government, then about to be made. And if, as we think, this was felt to be the alternative, how far, in view of the "weakness of the flesh," the circumstances justify the conclusion, we cannot take it upon us to say; but on the supposition that, with all the facts before them, it was felt to be the alternative, that it was entitled to some weight, no sane mind will deny. For doubtless, when we look at the question in all its bearings, it will be admitted that it was better for the experiment to be made, with this exception to the rule, than not to have been made at all.

As it appears to us, there is another difficulty of considerable moment connected with this subject, and which, with the light we now have, we dare not overlook in its examination; which is, that by public law, slaves being known as goods and chattels, and, as such, liable for the debts of their owners or masters, and on the faith of such public law, the owners of such slaves have doubtless obtained credits to a large amount which they could not have obtained, only for the security guaranteed in this species of property; that the government should, and if they would do right must, in their emancipation provide for such emergency. It may, and doubtless will be objected, that the owners have not, and cannot by the laws of nature have, any right of property in them. This has already been admitted, as will be remembered by the careful reader; but according to public law they have a right of property, and on the faith of this law, by common usage and consent, they, as an article of property, have been taken into the account as securities for the liabilities contracted. We frankly admit that the case is a deplorable one; but it exists as the fault of the law; and the governments cannot, without the most heartless mockery of public justice, back out from their responsibilities in this matter.

That it is our duty, partly on the grounds of public justice, and partly on the principles of moral goodness, to meet these emergencies, and others that may possibly exist which have escaped our attention, will not, and, as we think, cannot be denied. For the time is coming, and we trust is not far distant, when our duty in a public or civil point of view in this particular, as well as in our social and individual capacities, must be looked at in the light and principles of Christianity. Their practical utility on this, as well as on all other subjects, will, by the force of its own intrinsic excellence and power, commend itself to public notice, and wrest from the nation the homage due to truth. Such long has been, and such especially, as we think, in a partial degree, under its powerful workings at the present time, to be the tone of public sentiment; that a great solicitude is felt as to what is the best course to overcome it, and what is the best disposition that can be made of it, to make it a boon to all concerned; which brings us to offer some thoughts on this aspect of the question.

Our views on this subject, with some little qualifications and exceptions, cannot be better, if so well expressed, as we find them in the language of the late

Richard Watson: "As to the existence of slavery in Christian States, every government, as soon as it professes to be Christian, binds itself to be regulated by the New Testament; and though a part of its subjects should at that time be in a state of servitude, and their sudden emancipation might be obviously an injury to society at large, it is bound to show that its tendency is as inimical to slavery, as the Christianity which it professes. All the injustice and oppression against which it can guard that condition, and all the mitigating regulations it can adopt, are obligatory upon it; and since also every Christian slave is enjoined by apostolic authority to choose freedom, when it is possible to attain it, as being a better state, and more befitting a Christian man, so is every master bound, by the principle of loving his neighbour, and especially his 'brother in Christ,' as himself, to promote his passing to that better and more Christian state. To the instruction of such slaves in religion, would every such Christian government also be bound, and still further to adopt such measures for the final extinction of slavery; the rule of its proceeding in this case being the accomplishment of its object as soon as is compatible with the real welfare of the enslaved portions of the subjects themselves, and not the consideration of the losses which might be sustained by their proprietors, which, however, ought to be compensated by other means, as far as they are just and equitably estimated.

"If this be the mode of proceeding, clearly pointed out by Christianity, to a state on its first becoming Christian, when previously, for ages, the practice of slavery had grown up with it, how much more forcibly does it impose its obligations upon nations involved in the guilt of modern African slavery! They professed Christianity when they commenced the practice. They entered upon a traffic which, *ab initio*, was, upon their own principles, unjust and cruel. They had no rights of war to plead against the natural rights of the first captives, who were in fact stolen, or purchased from stealers, knowing them to be so. The governments themselves never acquired any right in the parents; they have none in their descendants, and can acquire none; as the thief who steals cattle cannot, should he feed and defend them, acquire any right of property either in them or the stock they may produce, although he should be at the charge of rearing them. These governments, not having a right of property in their colonial slaves, could not transfer any right of property in them to their present masters, for it could not give what it never had, nor, by its connivance at the robberies and purchases of stolen human beings, alter the essential injustice of the transaction. All such governments are, therefore, clearly bound, as they fear God and dread his displeasure, to restore all their slaves to the condition of freedom. Restoration to their friends and country is now out of the question; they are bound to protect them where they are, and have the right to exact their obedience to good laws in return; but property in them they cannot obtain,—their natural right to liberty is untouched and inviolable. The manner in which this right is to be restored, we grant, is in the power of such governments to determine, provided that proceeding be regulated by the principles above laid down:—First, that the emancipation be sincerely determined upon at some time future; secondly, that it be not delayed beyond the period which the general interest of the slaves themselves prescribes, and which is to be judged of benevolently, and without any bias of judgment, giving the advantage of every doubt to the injured party. Thirdly, that all possible means be adopted to render freedom a boon to them. It is only under such circumstances that the continuance of slavery among us can cease to be a national sin, calling down, as it has done, and must do, until a process of emancipation be honestly commenced—the just displeasure of God. What compensation may be justly claimed from the governments, that is, the public of those countries who have entangled themselves in this species of unjust dealing, by those who have purchased men and women whom no one had a right to sell, and no one had a right to buy, is a perfectly distinct question, and ought not to turn repentance and justice out of their course, or delay their operations for a moment. Perhaps such is the unfruitful nature of all wrong, that it may be found, that as free labourers, the slaves would be of equal or more value to those who employ them than at present. If otherwise, as in some degree 'all have sinned,' the real loss ought to be borne by all, when that loss is fairly and impartially ascertained; but of which loss, the slave interest, if we may so call it, ought in justice to bear more than an equal share, as having had the greatest gain."—*Theol. Inst.*, vol. iii, p. 273.

These paragraphs, according to a note appended by the American editors, which is doubtless true, were obviously written with a view to states in which Christianity, as a system, is formally established by law. That does not, however, materially alter the question in their application to us. For if religion with us is not, and, as we think, ought not to be established by law, we are, nevertheless, as a people, professedly Christian. It being the popular, and, with very limited exceptions, the only religion known among us. And as we, the people, in the form of government, are established the sovereigns in this country, the principles and arguments contained in the above quotation apply to us in all their force, with the exceptions we take to the following sentence: "Restoration to their friends and country is now out of the question." Restoration to their friends may have been out of the question; but the correctness of its being out of the question to restore them to their country, may be honestly doubted. True, the immense amount of the public debt of the British Government would have been an embarrassing question in its connexion with such an attempt. But if, as a government, they had had in this matter as much regard to public justice as they had for vain, ostentatious, and ambitious parade and show, by which to keep up the dignity and glory of the court of England, as evinced in the astounding dimensions of her civil list, this item, paired down to what is befitting, in view of this and other matters of public justice, would have gone far in the lapse of time in accomplishing their return to their own country.

Happily for us in this country, we are, by law, to a very great extent, free from the enormous burdens of their civil list; and by an economical administration of the government, may soon be free from any public debt. And with the inexhaustible resources of our country, especially in view of our late acquisitions, and which could not be more worthily appropriated, we might address ourselves to this work with every prospect, in the lapse of time, of complete success. And how nobly and godlike would it look, for a nation actuated by a high sense of public justice and moral goodness, thus magnanimously to repair its own, and the wrongs of others.

And this, after all we have read and heard to the contrary, when we look at the subject in all its bearings, as well as in the light of God's moral and providential government of the world, seems to us to be the one indicated by Providence, and the best disposition that can be made of it.

The prejudice of colour in itself, not to say that it possibly may be designed as a providential barrier, is so deeply rooted, that the probability is strong against their ever attaining fully to the rights of citizenship in this country, while the history of nations furnishes evidence that two distinct and separate nations or races cannot co-exist on the same soil,—the stronger preying upon the weaker, and the weaker thereby tending to decay. And it is not rational to suppose that amalgamation will ever overcome the evil. Therefore, having full confidence in the practicability of the measure, we believe colonization to be the best; and, as above stated, the one indicated by Providence. And if it is, as we have assumed, and frequently stated it to be, the duty of our General and State Governments, on principles of public justice and moral goodness, to make the earliest practical provision for the emancipation of our coloured population—having proper reference to their interest in so doing, it cannot be their duty to make provision for its further extension and perpetuation. This would be to confound all distinctions with regard to the rule of duty, and involve the State and national councils in the most positive contradiction; so much so, that the most unlettered citizen of this great republic could clearly see their incongruity.

The question, then, resolves itself either into the rightfulness of slavery, or the expediency of its longer continuance, and its further extension, as necessary in view of such continuance.

The doctrine of its rightfulness has already been sufficiently refuted; for, as we have seen, both the law of nature and the law of revelation lift up their united voice in its condemnation. And we need not insult the reader's understanding by any further effort to disprove the rightfulness of its claims.

We have already stated that, in a political point of view, the earliest practicable attention in their emancipation and removal, having reference to the good of the enslaved, is the measure of our obligation to them. On this principle would it not be safe in five, or at furthest ten, years—or sooner, if practicable—for our national and State governments to commence operations in this glorious and God-like movement. Hopefully, not to say certainly, in that time, or even before that time, matters and things, in reference to this question, could be got in that state of matured preparation which is necessary to, and should characterize, the incipient measures in this movement.

If so, the next question which arises in this connexion is, whether there is, in those States where the relation now exists by municipal law, sufficient room for their comfortable accommodation, for the period of time above stated. To propose this question is to answer it; it being obviously true that there is abundance of room for them, even for a much longer period of time. For, in addition to the room there is in the old, and a number of the comparatively new slaveholding States, Texas itself furnishes a sufficient space for the increase of our coloured population for half a century to come.

And furthermore, the advocates for the extension of slavery have never felt this to be a difficulty, and therefore have never set up the plea of necessity for more room; but, in our federal relations, have claimed it as a matter of right, guaranteed to them by the constitution of the general government. Now, according to these facts, the doctrine of expediency is not tenable on this ground.

And we suppose it will not be pretended that it is necessary, in view of the supposed advantages that a new settlement, in a new country, will furnish, for their physical, mental, and moral culture, preparatory to their emancipation. This, as it seems to us, would be advancing backwards.

So far as national policy is concerned, it would doubtless be most desirable to have harmonious national action in the settlement of this question. And it is to be hoped that the South will yet see and retract their error in insisting on its further extension. If they should not, what in this exigency is the duty of the North?

If, as we have seen, slavery is in derogation of the law of nature, and also of the spirit and principles of Christianity, and only tolerated in the Divine administration for the time being, in view of the "weakness of the flesh," till the practical benefits of the gospel should, in their development, prepare the way and point out the path of duty, ought they longer to co-operate with the South, by lending their sanction to the extension and indefinite perpetuation of this wrong—this curse of humanity, and reproach of this nation? We repeat, can they do so, without incurring, at the bar of a world's opinion, the verdict of a world's condemnation? And, what is immeasurably worse, can they do so without falling under the displeasure, and bringing down upon this guilty nation the fearful judgments, of the almighty Ruler of the universe, who assures us that he hates oppression, and will in the end, in behalf of the oppressed, terribly vindicate right?

SECTION V.

A CALM ADDRESS TO THE SOUTH.

When from afar-off ages or generations the history of a people, in all the force of their educational associations and biases, is written in deep and palpable wrongs, on the known laws of mind they have claims on our sympathy, and we cannot act rationally in withholding it from them. If, in connexion with this, these wrongs, from the commencement of their political history, have been authorized by public law, as a part and parcel of the civil and social state, their claims on our sympathy are strengthened. Added to this, that what is regarded as their sacred writings have many tolerant allusions to, and directions for, the management of those wrongs as elements of civil, social, and religious society,—those claims are increased by all the force of the over-awing and down-bearing tendency of so high authority; which, with beings constituted as we are, in whom the religious principle is one of the strongest of our nature, must necessarily be great, and cannot fail to make a deep and lasting impression, one to which the mind cleaves with great tenacity;—watching with feelings of profound jealousy every attempted innovation on established and long-cherished opinions and usages, and only surrendering them to the most clear, conclusive, and obvious reasons of right and fitness. They must be clear, in opposition to cloudy or murky; conclusive, in opposition to "doubtful disputations;" obviously out-standing, so as to commend themselves to our intelligence as being free from hypothetical conjectures, rhetorical flourishes, and every species of illusory reasoning, by which to impose upon the understanding by false appearances, however plausibly presented. If there is a lurking sentiment within, that the arts of sophistry have been employed, and the case not both fairly and fully met, the mind, instead of being staggered from its former position, cleaves with renewed confidence and satisfaction to the stability of its old and cherished opinions.

Now with these known facts of the laws of mind before us, how would we, supposing they were heathen, approach a people situated as above described? In the language of coarse, vulgar, inflammatory, wholesale denunciation; consigning them to immeasurable infamy in the present life, and to the miseries of an endless hell in the life to come? What law of mind, or principle of human nature, warrants even the shadow of a conclusion that we shall make a favourable impression, or bring about a reformation by such a course? We must confess that we have wholly misinterpreted human nature, in its mental, moral, and social tendencies, if such a course, instead of being productive of favourable results, will not tend to harden and confirm them in those wrongs, and thus render more difficult, if not totally defeat, for the time being, the meliorating object contemplated.

If this reasoning holds good in its application to heathen nations, what reason have we to depart from it in its application to Christian nations? Are the laws of mind, and the principles of human nature, so changed by the accidental or providential circumstances of our existence, as to render effectual in the latter case that course which proved an entire failure in the former? By what process of reasoning can we arrive at such a conclusion? There is none of which we can form the most distant conception. And yet, as it appears to us, in the manner we approach the South on the subject of slavery, this whole question is begged—taken for granted. The cases are to all intents and purposes analogous; the South being similarly situated in reference to slavery, as the heathen nation in the wrongs above supposed. True, there have been repeated and successful efforts to prove slavery a great wrong; the laws of nature have been summoned to the bar of public opinion, and have uttered, in unmistakable testimony, their verdict of condemnation; but a remark before made may be here repeated, that weak and ineffectual is its testimony, while there is a lurking sentiment within, that a higher authority has authorized it. Mankind do not go to the laws of nature, but to the Bible, to learn the rules of moral duty; and so long as from that source they can derive any support for the principle or practice of slavery, the laws of nature will, as a general matter, be appealed to, and lift up their voice in vain on this question. But the Bible has also been appealed to. Admitted. But after what manner? Alas! here, where all should be clear, conclusive, and out-standing, there has been the greatest darkness, doubt, and confusion.

Some have taken and laid down general principles from the Bible, and drawn conclusions from those principles antagonistic to slavery; and gravely tell us, whatever might have been the state of this question in the earlier and darker ages of the Church and the world, that now the relation is utterly incompatible with Christianity; forgetting or overlooking, in the mean while, the great cardinal doctrine of Divine revelation, that the Scriptures were not given for one race, or for one time, but for all races, and for all time.

Others, starting from these general principles, unheedingly ride over the whole class of Scriptures which, by tolerant allusion, and specific law, recognize the relation, and give directions for its management, as an element of civil, social, and religious society.

Others, again, attempt, but in a manner so weak and unsatisfactory, to criticise and explain away those passages that bear directly on the relation, that the veriest blockhead of a school-boy, twelve or fifteen years of age, who can comprehend the ideas of which language is the sign, can detect their fallacy.

Others, finding it impossible to give any rational explication of those passages, only in their application to a state of slavery; and being unable to reconcile the tolerant recognition of the relation with their views of the character and government of God, renounce the Bible as a Divine revelation, and launch out into the wide and open fields of infidelity and skepticism.

While others, with better accredited reputation for general learning and intelligence, and equal claims to common honesty, common sense, and consistent piety with the best of them, regard those Scriptures as bearing upon the relation, and the relation as compatible with a creditable profession of religion, on the part of both master and servant.

So that amidst these conflicting views, asserted with equal zeal and confidence, an Egyptian darkness enshrouds the question, doubt is induced, and, on the principles above laid down, the mind which has been trained by the whole force of its education, from infancy to manhood, to certain modes of thinking on this subject, settles down in the conclusion, that after all the elemental strife that has sounded in its ears, and after all the war of doubtful disputation to which it has given attention, it still is in the right, and therefore proceeds forward in the beaten track of ages.

Now it does appear to us that this is the exact, the true state of this question—the necessary result of the unadvised or the ill-advised manner in which the investigation of this subject has been conducted. Hence the bold and out-standing position of certain eminent Southern men, in contending for slavery as a Bible institution, challenging controversy on its rightfulness, &c. We repeat, while the question retains this shape, and nothing more clear and definite, with regard to its true position in the Divine administration, is elicited, this whole matter of vehement, reproachful, and unmeasured denunciation is useless, and worse than useless: it is both irrational and un-Christian. It might be employed with a faint shadow of plausibility among hog-drovers, in driving their stock to market; but in no sense of the word whatever is it admissible among rational, intelligent, morally free, and accountable men.

We are aware that in these remarks we shall call down upon ourselves like denunciations from certain ignorant praters, or "filthy dreamers," who know better how to use their pens and tongues in coarse, vulgar, and slanderous reproach, than they do about the principles and spirit of Christianity; but, supported by a deep, inward, conscious desire of promoting only the truth, it is a light thing with us "to be judged" and reviled "of men," and especially by such men.

We have already been interrogated as to the latitude for which the book was written,—a question that jaundiced prejudice, impertinent or well-meant ignorance, might ask; but one that no intelligent and upright mind, actuated by the principles and spirit of Christianity, could ask. It could not dabble in such dirty water, or swim in such a muddy stream, for the plain and obvious reason, that pure Christianity impugns no man's motives, and particularly in an act so public and solemn as that of writing and publishing a book on any great moral question. Therefore they excite our pity, rather than our contempt.

We repeat: That before we can rationally expect to make any favourable impression, or gain a candid and impartial hearing in the court of the Southern understanding, we must change our whole mode of attack,—"turning our swords into plough-shares, and our spears into pruning-hooks;" indicating thereby the double purpose of yielding our hostile ground, and in a peaceful, quiet, patient, but persevering way, digging deep into the soil of revealed truth, till we fathom the depths of the Divine administration, and ascertain, if possible, and as far as possible, the true position of this feature of its policy.

This, to some extent, has been the design of the

present effort; in which we have endeavoured to trace its connexion with the moral and providential government of God; and which we may here recapitulate, for the twofold purpose of placing the question in as clear and distinct point of light as may be, and as affording rational ground of appeal to all concerned, with regard to duty in the premises.

First. That the constitution of human nature is such, that civil government is not only indicated as being necessary, but is revealed as being the will of God, and is essential to the existence of the race.

Second. That in view of its lying so deep at the foundation of our existence, the Church, which can only exist, and is only necessary, in the continued existence of the race, is, particularly under the Gospel dispensation, subordinate in her position, and subject to the laws of the State in every matter where those laws do not directly conflict with the law of God—as in the case of Daniel, &c.

Third. That in the moral and providential government of God, the race is continued in existence in a fallen, disordered, and mixed condition.

Fourth. That if it was just in God to continue the race in existence in their fallen, disordered, and mixed condition, the very same justice required that a benevolent regard be had to the circumstances under which we exist.

Fifth. That this benevolent regard is shown in the slavery relation, in its tolerant recognition for the time being; because, first, it could be turned to the spiritual advantage of those in the relation, under the patriarchal and Jewish dispensations; and, second, that under the Gospel dispensation, from the known hostility of the parties, a law forbidding it by direct positive precept would, in the agitations of universal war and bloodshed that would have followed its announcement and enforcement, have been a greater calamity to the race than its temporary toleration. And especially in view of the vigilance of Providence in turning it to good account, as a lesson of instruction to all created intelligences, on the painfully unnatural and deeply evil character of sin; as well as a measure of providential government that has already been—spiritually and otherwise—and yet may be much more so, of vast importance to Africa itself.

Sixth. That its tolerant recognition is only in view of the "weakness of the flesh," or present disordered state of the world.

Seventh. That this tolerant recognition of the relation, as a temporary regulation, is guarded by restrictions and regulations which are promotive of the best interests of all who are providentially found in that relation, both for time and eternity.

Eighth. That it is essential wickedness to attempt by force or fraud to reduce a free man to a state of bondage.

Ninth. That as men, or Christians, we are justified in continuing in the relation only so long as we are unavoidably ignorant of its true position, and the reasons of its toleration in the government of God, or connected with it by the operation of laws or circumstances which we did not create, and cannot control, and which laws or circumstances render emancipation a doubtful good.

Tenth. That it is our duty, both as citizens and Christians, to seek by all constitutional, orderly, and peaceful measures, to remove all those legal and moral barriers which prevent their emancipation.

This, so far as they now occur to us, .is a brief analysis of the important principles elaborated in this investigation, and which, as we think, show the very complex and delicate nature of the relation;—the reasons for, and the extent to which it is tolerated;—with the circumstances under which we are not and are justifiable in continuing in the relation, as well as our solemn duty, whether as citizens or Christians, to seek, in a proper way, its removal. And the whole question, as it appears to us, is disabused from its darkness, doubt, and confusion, and the path of duty plain before us.

And how, with these facts before them, and other equally reliable and outstanding facts connected with this question, (to which attention has been called,) a body of grave, learned, and magnanimous divines could, in grave deliberation, solemnly determine to sever the bonds of visible, fraternal, and Christian unity of a large and prosperous Church, for the sake of sustaining a bishop, who, contrary at least to implied faith, had connected himself with this evil, is to us as inexplicable as the tides, on any other principle than on their part a total misconception and misapprehension of the facts here stated, and which are legitimate deductions from revelation, reason, and the debates of the General Conference, before alluded to. The principles of Christian charity are such, that if it even was in our heart to do so—which we utterly disclaim—we dare not charge them with known dereliction of principle in the course they have pursued in this matter. It is capable of other, and more worthy and rational explanations. Facts warrant us in a different interpretation of their course. Many of them claim that it is a Bible institution, an appointment of

God. How generally this sentiment prevails, we have not the means of definite knowledge; but it is rational to conclude, that the fogs and mists under which they have been accustomed to view this question, have had much to do in misleading them.

Again: public sentiment in the South, by these misleading causes, lay in this direction; and how far they may have felt themselves bound to regard that public sentiment, doubtless came in for a full share of their sober regard.

And yet again, as they claim their professedly conventional rights, as an integral portion of the Church this may have, and doubtless, from the debates of the General Conference, had, a great deal to do with the course adopted. We repeat, on the supposition that they have had no such clearly defined and settled views as we think are here presented, and as we believe are presented in the Scriptures, but have taken the views above intimated; these form rational and consistent grounds for explaining what we believe to be, and will here call, their erratic course, without ungenerously and unchristianly impugning their motives; a principle that stands at an immeasurable distance from that charity which "rejoices not in iniquity, but rejoices in the truth, beareth all things, believeth all things, hopeth all things."

What course they will subsequently pursue, when clearer light and better defined views shall mark the boundaries, and fix the distinct limits of this question, the future must determine. But that they can cling to it in the sense of Divine right, Divine appointment, or an institution of God, seems to us to be utterly out of the question. For if the views we have presented in these pages be Scriptural, and the contrary we think no man can prove, on their high, holy, and unerring authority, there is not even the shadow of evidence to sustain such claims. The very strongest Scriptural view that can be taken of it is, that through the Divine forbearance it is temporarily tolerated; not because it is right in the sense of eternal rectitude, or the laws of nature, but in view of the ignorance, weakness, and disordered state of the world, which it is their business, as the ministers of a religion of essential moral goodness, to labour to correct —a moral goodness so essentially disinterested and self-sacrificing, that instead of putting its feet on the neck of the poor, oppressed, and down-trodden ones, would, like an angel of mercy, fly to their rescue, and say, in the language of Him who is their pattern and head, "The Spirit of the Lord is upon me, because he hath anointed me to preach the gospel to the poor, he hath sent me to heal the broken-hearted, to preach deliverance to the captives, and recovering of sight to the blind; to set at liberty them that are bruised, to preach the acceptable year of the Lord." The poor, the outcast, the oppressed, the bound, and crushed,— in a word, the neglected masses of society—were those with whom the blessed Jesus sympathized and laboured, for whom he lived, and for whom he died. Under the quickening power of a moral goodness, which, at the sight of their deep woes and deeper wrongs, stirred the fires of divinity within him, He came from heaven to earth to lift them up to their proper elevation here, and eternal glory hereafter. And can his representatives, his ambassadors, charged with all the interests of his great mission, not only to the fallen, but to the most deeply fallen, unfortunate, helpless, and distressed, so far forget their true position, as to sustain a bishop who has given the whole weight of his spiritual and official character to sustain and perpetuate that state of things which the great Master came to subvert, uproot, and bear down, until man's true dignity and common brotherhood should, throughout his entire history, be practically asserted and realized? Or having, in the unexpected hour of hurried excitement, thus touched the ark of God with an unsteady hand, will they, in their more cool deliberation, when sober second thoughts hold empire, through pride of opinion, or any other unworthy motive, continue in a wrong position? Would it be magnanimous? Would it be Christian or Christ-like to do so? But you reply, We misinterpret your position, and disclaim any such intention on the part of yourselves or your bishop. We rejoin, What is the sound that has, from the South, gone forth to the world on this question? Is it not that slavery is of Divine authority, and therefore right?—right for every minister and bishop to have slaves—that it is essential to the usefulness of a minister in the South to be a slaveholder? With many other similar expressions, which all conspire to fix it as the opinion of the Southern ministry, that it is an essential and permanent element of civil, social, and religious society; and all this without one solitary breathing whisper that we have ever heard or seen of its temporary character, and only in the Divine forbearance tolerated in that sense, in view of the "weakness of the flesh," or for want of a sufficient amount of moral goodness in principle and practice by which to overthrow it; or, in other words, because the balance of power on this question was on the wrong side—the side of sin, the side of the devil; and that in that early, dark, heathenish age of the world, to have arrayed those powers in conflict, by a direct positive law forbidding slavery, would have been a greater calamity to mankind than its temporary toleration. We repeat, that under the gospel dispensation this is the most palpable reason that can be assigned for its toleration. And when we hear without a dissenting whisper a sound like the seven last thunders, coming up from the whole South, that it is a Bible institution, and as such to take permanent rank among the positive duties of society, are we to be told that we misinterpret them when we say that in their action in this matter the whole weight of their influence is on the wrong side—the side of sin—the side of the devil,—perfectly antagonistic to what it should and must be, if they would increase that balance of power, or moral goodness, which, on this subject, is to give the preponderance on the side of right, of truth, of humanity, and of Christ? Impossible! It is too unmistakably true in its practical consequences to admit of one moment's doubt. Whatever may be the amount of their disclaimers, mankind will read in this action, and their position consequent upon that action, a broad sanction to the principle and practice of slavery.

That in their action they designed a contravention of the principles of moral goodness, or to be on the wrong side of the balance of power, is another and distinct question. As already stated, we do not, we dare not, impugn their motives. Facts, out and long-standing facts, viz.: the as yet unmet challenge given by the South to four of our most learned doctors of the North, to discuss the sinfulness of slavery, compels us to believe that they honestly regard themselves in the right. But we think, and must contend, that by the weight of all the facts, principles, and arguments elaborated in this investigation, we are borne out in the conclusion, that in their zeal to do right they have done wrong, which it is their imperious duty, on being convinced thereof, without let or hindrance, to retract, by correcting their position before the world.

Shall we attempt further arguments with our brethren of the Church South? And can we do so, avoiding the beaten track which, on this subject, has filled their ears, from the earliest agitation of this question? These are already before them, and need not be here repeated further than to say, that however irrational and unchristian we may, and do, regard the manner, yet the matter of many of those arguments, appeals, &c., embody correct principles; principles that ought not, could not, and would not, have been disregarded, had they been presented in a proper manner. And the South, on this subject, should, even at these unseemly, and, as to manner, unbefitting calls, awake from the slumber of ages, moved thereto by the following known laws of human nature:

First. That such is our mental and moral constitution, that we cannot adopt any principle, or engage in any practice, true or false, right or wrong, and continue therein any considerable length of time, without finding a tendency, both mentally and morally, to become satisfied with, or easy in our position. In the outset we may have our most serious doubts, possibly our clear convictions, of both the incorrect and injurious character of such principle, or rule of action, and fall painfully under the displeasure of conscience in embracing the one, or acting upon the other; yet in adopting the theory, or acting upon the rule for a time, matters become most seriously changed. Conscience, conviction, and doubt, are all gone; and soon the mind, thus agitated at the threshold of this new era in our history, rights over to the at first doubted, convicted, and conscience-smitten position; and as a general matter, feels as dead to any other sensation than that of ease and complacency, as if it was conscious of the most essential rectitude. This ease and complacency may be attributed to the silence imposed upon our mental and moral powers, by the act of receiving and entertaining principles and practices at variance with their dictates, rather than to their approval of such theory or practice. Granted. But does not the existence of the conceded fact prove the truth of our proposition, that such is the tendency of mind? And it matters not, so far as the practical consequences are concerned, whether the state of mind induced by the reception and practice of error consists in simple inaction, or a real and essential perversion of its tendency to wrong. The end is reached, and all the fearful consequences involved in that end.

But we are inclined to the opinion, that facts warrant the conclusion, and we think the Scriptures sustain the doctrine, that such is our mental and moral constitution, that the embrace and practice of error produces in us a real and proportionate tendency to the side of wrong; and which grows with our growth, and strengthens with our strength, until the character is finished for good or ill, as the case may be; for the rule works both ways. And thus every additional step taken in a course of error, destroys our aptitude to, and power to do right, and proportionately increases the power of evil over us.

This principle, or law of our nature, is strikingly exemplified in the inebriate, the highwayman, the murderer, and every other shade and shape of progressive vice; each renewed act of intemperance, or violence, diminishing our power of resistance, and increasing the evil forces within us; all of which our own observation, together with the living and dying confessions of our fellow-men, abundantly confirm.

And this tendency of our nature is forcibly expressed by Pope:

> "Vice is a monster of so frightful mien,
> As to be hated, needs but to be seen;
> But seen too oft, familiar with her face,
> We first endure, then pity, then embrace."

And its power over us, as the result of long habit or indulgence, is fearfully portrayed in the language of the prophet Jeremiah: "Can the Ethiopian change his skin, and the leopard his spots? then may ye also do good who are accustomed to do evil." So that it is clear that the frequent repetition of wrong, or a long continuance in error, has the tendency to induce habits the will cannot resist, and finally, for aught we can see to the contrary, to become an unalterable part and parcel of our mental and moral constitution. This, as it appears to us, is the doctrine of the Holy Scriptures, as taught in the following passages:

"And for this cause (because they received not the love of the truth) God shall send them strong delusions, that they should believe a lie that they all might be damned." And again, "And for this cause, God gave them up unto vile affections," &c.

Now we suppose these passages are similar in their import, and, at least, intimate the downward tendency of human nature in its erratic course, and the fearful acme gained in the progress of error, that they are abandoned of heaven, left to their own waywardness, to work out their own destruction with greediness. And how frequently, in the single sin of drunkenness, do we witness the verity of these solemn and awful declarations; and which, so far as time or the present life is concerned, abundantly sustains the truth of our proposition, relative to the laws of mimd. And we have, at least, one passage that reflects some light on this subject, in its application to eternity. It is the narrative of the rich man and Lazarus. Now it is clear from the history of the case, as here given, that the rich man, in his life-time, had Moses and the prophets, but, disregarding their instructions as a rule of duty, he lived a man of the world. When he died he found himself in hell; and having no hope in his own case, his sympathies were drawn out in behalf of his brethren he had left behind him; and he desired that Lazarus might be sent to warn them, lest they also come into that place of torment. He was told they had Moses and the prophets, let them hear them. And he said, "Nay, father Abraham, but if one went unto them from the dead they would repent." So that he appears to have carried his bad principles and determined opposition to the Divine government to hell with him; and though enveloped in its flames, and feeling in his own experience the fearful demonstration of its verity, maintained those principles, and that opposition, in a controversy with father Abraham; so that on the high and unerring authority of Scripture, as well as the laws of mind, as above explained, however we may account for it, the incessant changes of character, constantly going on in the history of man in the present life, tend to, and finally terminate in, an unchangeable, an unalterable character.

It may be inquired, what is meant by all this? What relevancy have these remarks on the laws of mind and morals, to the question in hand? We answer, much, very much. They may put us on our guard in the investigation of all moral questions,—a precaution of immense importance on any moral subject. And what moral question is there of greater moment than the one involved in these pages,—the right and the practice of slavery,—a slavery in which millions of human beings are, by force of existing civil laws, doomed, from generation to generation, and from century to century, to pass a mere animal existence; crushed in body, crushed in mind, crushed in morals; in a word, crushed in every ennobling aspiration and feature of humanity,—in everything that indicates their high origin, as having been made in the image of God,—in everything that renders life desirable, or existence worth the name,—crushed in life, crushed in death, crushed in time, and crushed in eternity? Not there, however, in the sense of ultimate perdition, as the necessary result of their present degradation. But if the law of analogy holds good, in its application to the future world, their faculties and powers will have had so little development in the present life, as preparatory to the more enlarged, elevated, and refined enjoyments of the heavenly state, as to be in heaven, should they get there, mere infants, as compared to men. And may we not, yea, ought we not, to suspect the soundness of that mind, which in its reasonings and conclusions has adopted views favourable to the principles and practice of a system so down-bearing and imbruting in its tendency; and which, with feelings of complacency, can witness its operations, and the effect of its operations, as being under the misleadings of error? Is it not rational to suppose that this complacency, so far from being the result of well-defined views or clear convictions of its rightfulness, is the result of human selfishness, strengthened by such familiarity with the wrongs of slavery as to stifle our sense of right, and by this effect of error on our mental and moral constitution, dry up our sympathies for, and leave us thus indifferent with regard to its wrongs? And if so, ought we not to recur to first principles; examine the ground over again, and on rational and Scriptural principles, be able to satisfy ourselves, as men, that we are correct in our position? It can do no harm. Truth and right never suffer by the closest scrutiny. And, on the other hand, it may do good; for it is a well-known truth, that we are often benefited by subjecting ourselves, and our principles, to the closest scrutiny and most rigid examination. And by what process of reasoning can we arrive at the conclusion, that a course that will be productive of good results on all other questions will be unavailing in this? There is none.

And however we may feel settled and satisfied with the existing state of things on the question of slavery, there is one strong ground of suspicion that we may be in the wrong. And that is, the opinion of the world is on the other side of the question. And it cannot be that the laws of mind are so essentially different, that we must be conducted to conclusions on this subject so wide apart. The Scriptures inform us, that the principles of moral rectitude therein found constitute the rule, or law, by which all nations are to be judged. This, in reference to the great question of morals, is conclusive of the unity of mind. True, all minds may not equally comprehend moral questions, either primarily or in detail. One reason we might offer for this difference is, the diversity of talent possessed by mankind; one having five, another two, and another one talent. Another reason may be, that some men exercise their powers more than others in the investigation of such questions. But all this does not affect the question. Moral truth is one, and the moral powers of the race are alike, at least in nature, adapted to that truth. And what the moral intelligence of the world determines to be wrong, that verdict, when sustained by the laws of nature and the laws of God, as in the case of slavery, must be true.

Another thought of some importance to the impartial examination of this subject is, that those connected with slavery are interested witnesses. And such is the importance attached to this principle, in matters pertaining to the well-being of society, that in all well-defined and well-settled systems of civil jurisprudence, the testimony of such witnesses is inadmissible, only under circumstances, the nature of which preclude the possibility of other or better testimony. And ought it not to be taken into the account, in the settlement of this question? Can we, in view of the weakness of human nature, without giving the injured party the full benefit of this tendency of human nature to its own interest, decide fairly and impartially? We think not.

And, on such a subject, can a Christian people lightly disregard the sober judgment of the world, especially in view of the fact just stated, that their relation to it is such as to render them less interested, and therefore the more competent judges? Is it rational, is it Christian to do so? We maintain that no man can act either rationally or Christian-like who unheedingly and impatiently gives the go-by to, and disregards, the opinion of mankind on any question, and particularly on one of so grave importance as the question of slavery. True, it may be claimed that the evil is among yourselves, and that it is your own business to manage it. Granted. And we will here add, that we disclaim all right to interfere, in any way or manner, with your institutions, further than to appeal to your moral and religious sense, in the words of truth and soberness. This we may do, for we are all brethren. And the oppressed too are our brethren,—of the same blood,—children of a common parent, and all alike hastening to the same fearful or glorious end. It is in this broad view of our common origin, oneness, and destiny, that we would overleap the civil restrictions that hang around this question, and appeal to your sense of humanity, of right, and of grace. Can it be that an impartial and just God, who is loving to every man, and whose tender mercies are over all his works, is pleased with a system that thus imbrutes, from age to age, so many of his intelligent and accountable children? Can it be that He will not visit for these things? One guilty success after another may harden our feelings to the voice of humanity and truth. And we may conclude, as did ancient Israel, "that the vision is for many days to come, and the prophecy is of times afar off, and therefore, because judgment for an evil work is not speedily executed, go on in the work of oppression. But in this you err, not knowing the Scriptures, nor the power of God." For, in the language of the prophet, "The days are at hand, and the effect of every vision." That is, although the threatened doom may not be immediately visited, yet the cause is at work, and the effect as certainly realizing, in the moral process of iniquity that is going on within us, as if it were now upon us. Which brings us to the examination of another law of our nature, and one of great importance in this as well as all other moral questions.

It is as follows. That such is the delicacy of our mental and moral constitution, that we cannot inflict wrong, even in the slightest degree, without receiving wrong ourselves, in exact proportion to the wrong inflicted. Thus, when our mental and moral powers are properly adjusted, we cannot do wrong without a sense of personal meanness in proportion to the wrong done. It matters not whether done to a white man, a black man, or a brute. The sense of meanness is consequent upon the action. If the commission of outstanding and palpable wrong is not followed by a sense of meanness, it is conclusive of the perversion and corruption of those powers. And if, as sometimes is the case, we take pleasure in the wrong inflicted, and thus "glory in our shame," how total the change in our powers, and the ruin consequent upon that change! And to a mind that wishes to do right, is it not, and ought it not to be, a matter of the most serious interest, caution, and alarm, that such is the law of our nature, and such are the fearful consequences which necessarily follow its violation?

Now if, in the sense of essential rectitude, the principle and practice of slavery be wrong—in contravention of the laws of nature and the laws of God—it cannot fail to produce an unfavourable reaction on those who practise it, by disqualifying them for the perfection of moral government of which they were originally capable, and which Christianity seeks to restore. The Scriptures are a republication of those laws of nature; and the whole process of moral government, revealed in the Bible, is designed and calculated thus to lift us up. And just so far as it practically fails of this, it fails of the great object of its mission. And just so far as it accomplishes this, will it break down the principle and practice of slavery, and every other form of oppression. And it is as absolutely impossible for a man, be he bishop, priest, deacon, or layman, to be under the full renewing power of this wonderful scheme of human purification and elevation, and at the same time in principle and practice a slaveholder, as it is for him to be Christ and Belial at one and the same time. We may as well attempt to confound light and darkness, or destroy all distinctions between right and wrong, as to admit it; for the principles are essentially and eternally opposite: the one is from above, the other is from beneath; the one is from God, the other is from the devil. Mark! the question is not that even good men may not be in the relation, and so hedged about with circumstances, that, for the time being, it may be the best for them to continue in the relation. But it is impossible for a good man, fully imbued with the spirit of Christianity, to be at heart favourable to the system. With him, no consideration of ease, ambition, or gain, can weigh against the essential principles of right and goodness involved in the question. And how careful should a good man be, ay, how careful will he be, to guard himself against any connexion with the practical operation of a principle that is essentially and demonstrably from hell! And when we hear of Christian ministers pleading a connexion with it in view of their usefulness as ministers, and a grave bishop saying he believed God had called him to such a connexion, and that too in opposition to the known sense of his brethren, whose suffrage placed him in that spiritual elevation; we are strongly tempted to think there is some mistake in this business. There might have been a call. But if spiritual sensation had been in proper requisition, the odour of brimstone would have detected the cheat, and shown it to have come from the devil transformed into an angel of light, instead of from the "righteous Lord who loveth righteousness."

From the length of our remarks we are admonished to hasten to a close; and yet we can hardly tear ourselves away from the subject. The thought that it is possible for an intelligent community of nominal and professed Christians and Christian ministers, with the laws of nature before them, and the revelation of God, as a republication of those laws, in their hands, to undertake to defend the rightfulness and plead for the permanent continuance of the system of slavery, as being of special Divine appointment, is a heresy of such monstrous dimensions, that we may well denominate it high treason to nature, to revelation, to grace, and to God.

To effect their deliverance from their deep degradation, God has left as the work of the Church. If ever it be done, it is to be done by the power of Christian principle. Aside from this, there is no help, no hope for them. The sordid selfishness of human nature, its love of ambition, its love of ease, absolutely forbid all hope from this quarter. We may as rationally expect the father of lies to become devout, as to look to fallen human nature, which is essential wickedness, to take the lead in this movement of moral goodness. The Church then, as the depository of Christian sentiment, is the moral lever by which, on this subject, to move the world, and move it in the right direction; the source of light, to pour that flood of moral glory on the universal mind, which shall herald the jubilee of the oppressed and down-trodden. Should she prove recreant, and use that power to strengthen the reign of wrong and oppression, or suffer the light within her to become darkness, how profound the gloom, how terrific the picture of earth's deepest wrongs and deeper woes! Extinguish the light, strike down the principle and power of moral goodness revealed in the gospel, and what of hope is left for man? Lost! lost! lost! would be written on every heart; and the expiring throes of dying hope would convulse to its foundations our inmost being.

And are there no signs, no indications, no warning voice in the recent struggle and present position of the Southern Church, admonitory of this fearful tendency? Is there nothing connected with her history in this whole affair that speaks her on the side of wrong? These are questions of grave importance, and demand a corresponding answer. There should be no shuffling, no evasion, no exaggeration. The replication should be in the language of candour, soberness, and truth. Well, to their answer. That slavery is right, appointed by Jehovah, as a positive, permanent relation of society, distinctly and irrefragably capable of proof as such,—if such is the fact, then the South have done right in giving it their support. But we challenge the correctness of this position, and here affirm that no man can make good its pretensions to such claims. We think in these pages we have shown the contrary, beyond successful contradiction, and will thank any man, by fair, rational, and Scriptural argument, to disabuse us from such conviction. Were it not for seeming egotism, we would say we believe, we know it cannot be done. If it is not right, then it must of absolute necessity be wrong; there is no alternative. It is utterly out of the question to get away from this conclusion. But it is claimed that we have admitted the tolerant recognition of the relation, and laboured hard to prove its compatibility with the rectitude of the Divine character and government. Granted. But in what sense? Because it is right? Never, no never; or that those who are free from may run into it at their pleasure; no more than we could dare, voluntarily, to connect ourselves with any other outstanding and palpable wrong. The ground we have taken is simply this: that when a man, in the providence of God, is in it, under circumstances he did not create and cannot control, he is innocent; or when he connects himself with it, as an act of mercy, for the good of the slave. Under all other circumstances, supposing him to be properly informed on the subject, he is guilty of the sin of slavery, and of the wrong involved in that sin. We care not whether he be a bishop, a presiding elder, a preacher, or a layman. No position, no measure of fame, spiritually or otherwise, can shield him from the charge of guilt; and God, the judge of all, will hold him responsible, and require it at his hands.

In view of our love of ease, pleasure, honour, ambition, gain, and worldly glory, it may be convenient to marry a lady with a score of slaves, or by other methods receive or acquire them. But Jesus Christ and the apostles would no more have done so, than they would have joined an open and proclaimed alliance with hell. Everything we have on record of their history is demonstrative of this position. Then O, ye professed representatives, successors, and followers of Christ and the apostles; look on your exemplars, and feel the awkwardness of your position. How you have wounded them in the house of their friends! Don't blink the question! Awake from the dark sleep of slavery. Look big-souled gospel truth fully and squarely in the face; give conscience fair play, and doubtless you will see and feel your error.

Don't reason with flesh and blood, with ease, with pleasure, with ambition, with honour, with profit, or with worldly pomp and glory. But reason with truth, with right, with humanity, with God, with Christ. With Christ, when he said, "The spirit of the Lord is upon me, because he hath anointed me to preach the gospel to the poor; he hath sent me to heal the broken-hearted; to preach deliverance to the captives, and recovering of sight to the blind; to set at liberty them that are bruised." Reason with Christ in the garden, with Christ on the cross. Above all, reason with that moral goodness displayed in the salvation you teach, the religion you profess, the hope you entertain; which, but for the omnipotence of voluntary sin, would turn earth into paradise, and hell into heaven. And reconcile it if you can, on any other principles than those above laid down, with the principle and the practice of slavery.

Your plea of connexion with it, in view of the efficiency of the gospel ministry, is a vain philosophy, a false philosophy, the philosophy of the pit. It is to "do evil that good may come." A sad deterioration of the morals of the gospel, and a principle that no man can prove correct. Brother Winans may, if he can, write it in a sunbeam, or in the language of fire; but after all, to the intelligent mind, it amounts to this,—getting on to the platform of inebriation and mirth, to drink with the drunken, and frolic with the merry, and thus ingratiating ourselves into the graces of the worshippers in the temple of Bacchus, or at the shrine of sinful pleasure, that we may preach to them the gospel of Christ. In a word, it is "casting out devils by Beelzebub, the prince of devils." It is absolutely and eternally impossible, on the philosophy of gospel principles, to make anything else out of it. Brethren may talk and write, but, after all, it will only be talking and writing. All the bishops, and all the doctors of divinity and physic, and all the lawyers too, with senator Calhoun's aid into the bargain, cannot make good the principle, for the simple reason that truth is eternal, and lies on the other side of this question.

But you claim that the laws of the land have established the relation, that the Scriptures recognize their supremacy as the rule of duty in this matter; and, as citizens, it is your right to enjoy all the privileges guaranteed by the constitution and laws of your country. A question here arises: is the law which establishes slavery, as a social and civil relation, just? founded in such principles of right and fitness as to mark, unequivocally, its essential agreement with the laws of nature and the principles of moral rectitude, so as to vindicate its pretensions to the imposing character claimed in its behalf? And is it in view of this principle of right, that God's law takes hold of the relation? Or do the Christian Scriptures give it their temporary toleration as an element of the civil and social state, simply in view of the weakness of the flesh, bringing, at the same time, principles to bear upon, break it down, and crush it evermore? This, we maintain, is the true state of the question, and which we think is incontrovertibly sustained in these pages, and which is so manifestly the design of the gospel, that to deny it is virtually, yea, in verity, to reject the counsels of Heaven's mercy. And as above stated, it is the business of the Church to apply these correctives, to wage this war of moral power, on the principles of moral goodness, that the gospel, in this particular, may have free course, run and be glorified.

And how is she to do it? By trading in the bodies and the souls of men? or by the bishops and preachers marrying ladies that have a score or two of slaves on every convenient opportunity; and then, instead of using the influence of their position to mitigate their condition, and effect their liberation, do as bishop Andrew has done,—by deed of reconveyance to his wife, leave them in their slavery, and put it effectually out of his power to aid, Christlike, in the deliverance of the captives? and then, like the bishop, gravely tell us, that by this act they have washed their hands of the guilt of slavery? This may be true, so far as his hands are concerned; but we do not think it has washed his soul before God, or his position before the Church and the world, from blood-guiltiness. There is but one thing to protect him, and that is, unavoidable ignorance, which, if he or his friends can, they are at liberty to plead, in his behalf. But, we repeat, is the above the course the Church should take in fulfilling her mission of mercy to the world, for her bishops, preachers, and members, to monopolize all the slaves they can by marriage and otherwise; and thus give it their broad practical sanction, and then privately or publicly deplore it as a "great evil?" We think, by so doing they would fall under the whole weight of the apostle's castigation, contained in the following language: Rom. ii, 17–23. "Behold, thou art called a Jew, and restest in the law, and makest thy boast of God, and knowest his will, and approvest the things that are more excellent, being instructed out of the law, and art confident that thou thyself art a guide of the blind, a light of them which are in darkness, an instructor of the foolish, a teacher of babes, which hast the form of knowledge and of the truth in the law: thou therefore which teachest another, teachest thou not thyself? thou that preachest a man should not steal, dost thou steal? thou that sayest a man should not commit adultery, dost thou commit adultery? thou that abhorrest idols, dost thou commit sacrilege? thou that makest thy boast of the law, through breaking the law dishonourest thou God?"

But again, you claim your conventional rights, your rights as secured by the compromise laws, &c. With the controversy between the North and South on this subject we are not now concerned. It does not fall within the scope of our present object. But for the sake of argument, suppose, so far as the question of conventional rights is concerned, we concede all that the South claims, and to the full extent of those claims. Is not the principle involved in the issue between the parties—the rightfulness or sinfulness of the practice of slavery—of more importance than millions of such platforms, or more than all the interests involved in the controversy would be, supposing every minister in the entire South should lose his tiara in its triumphant vindication?

The fact is, when weighed in the balances of essential and eternal truth, there is no conceivable or inconceivable amount of conventional rights, which when, as in this case, are in contravention of the principle involved, that can by any possibility kick the beam. For the reasons just stated, these conventional rights, as the doings of men, are to "be shaken;" and the sooner the better. But the principle at stake is among "those things that cannot be shaken," and which must therefore "remain."

Such a contest about conventional rights, compromise laws, &c., might be expected from intriguing politicians, who do not study the science of government in the light of Christianity. But for a body of grave, learned Christian divines, full of godly wisdom, to contend for, and finally sever the bonds of a large, growing, prosperous Church, for the sake of sustaining them, is what we were not prepared to expect. We repeat: For the ministers of a Christianity which came from heaven to earth to lift up the most fallen, —not only as slaves, but as men, and as freemen, ("If thou mayest be made free, use it rather." "Be ye not therefore the servants of men,")—to crush the visible unity of a large and prosperous Church to sustain the practice of slavery, and thereby put to death this principle of moral goodness, or Christianity, is, in the history of such deliberations, a climax not often reached; and, in the course of our reading, without a parallel. Mark, we do not say that the South for the sake of it, as such, aimed at this consummation of iniquity. Nevertheless, such we believe to be the result. And we think they cannot get away from the conclusion.

But, further, they believe, they know that the North did not stand up to this question "unto the death" that followed, simply for the sake of oppressing them in their rights. We here venture to affirm that there is not a man of them who believes this; not one who, had this been the only light in which the North looked at this whole matter, but believes that the doings of the General Conference, so far as this question is concerned, would have passed off harmoniously.

The question with the North, then, was one of principle—of principle affecting conscience, which, if not the highest, is the most authoritative faculty of the human soul; one which, as they did, they should have abided, not only before the General Conference, the Church, and the world, but in the face of imprisonment and death.

Was the position of the South then, and is that position now, backed up and sustained by considerations of equal weight? Expediency was the ground then taken, and a pseudo expediency at that. There was no claim in the sense of unbending and eternal rectitude set up; conventional rights were pleaded,—rights based on an existing civil law, which is in contravention of the law of nature, and also of the law of God; and only, in the Divine administration, tolerated in view of the "weakness of the flesh" —the darkness, hardness, and mixed state of the world.

The North standing on a rock, the South over their eyes in the sand; the one planted on essential, immutable, eternal truth, and the other on expediency; now which is to surrender? which is to submit? We reply, that no amount or measure of expediency should or can set aside the claims of obvious moral principle. Paul's expediency did not strike down obvious moral principle; he was under no moral obligation to eat meat. And the expediency of the Gospel, in its tolerant recognition of the relation of slavery as a temporary regulation, does not strike down moral principle; it only comes to the aid of the "weakness of the flesh," by allowing us to continue in the relation so long as, in view of surrounding providential circumstances, it is positively the best that can be done with it; and thus enables us, by walking in or after its spirit, to fulfil the law, the paramount law of love, which works no ill to its neighbour, by holding him in chains when liberty is a practicable good. But the expediency for which they contend, which we have denominated a pseudo expediency, and which we here repeat, is one that provides for avoidable contingencies; and thus "makes provision for the flesh to fulfil the lusts thereof." Their bishop has lost his wife, who has left him a family of helpless children; he wants a wife and a mother for them. All right thus far. But he wants more,—some servants to nurse and wait on them. How convenient to marry a lady with a parcel of slaves, to do up this business!

The young preacher wants a wife, and how convenient to nest himself among half a dozen or more slaves, to wash and brush his clothes, to black his boots, to harness and take care of the horse, and to say "Massa," and to do up all "massa's" big and little turns! O how gratifying to the "lust of the flesh, the lust of the eye, and the pride of life!" This is the expediency for which they contend. Only read the debates of the General Conference, where they argue the constant liability of the Southern ministry to become connected with it by marriage and otherwise.

But there is another light in which they urge this doctrine of expediency, and which we wish here to examine a little. It is, if they submit to a deposed, dishonoured bishop, they would not dare to go home to their respective spiritual charges, or fields of ministerial labour. What is the reason of all this? What unread and unheard-of catastrophe would come upon them? Why, in the Southern States, including bishops, presiding elders, D. D's., and all, there are some three hundred thousand slaveholders, some of whom would be dreadfully put out with the doings of the General Conference in this matter. What portion of them? And who are they that would be so dreadfully torn to pieces, borne down, and crushed, or rather infuriated, by this act of the General Conference? Why, first of all, and foremost of all, high up in the very front ranks, is the Bishop himself; hard by his side, so far as the author has had the means of information, all the slaveholding members of the General Conference present. They all gave abundant evidence that they felt, and most deeply felt. But then the outbursting they manifested was only the reaction of the apprehended or real feeling at home, produced by the intelligence that had reached the distant South from the seat of the General Conference. Well, be it so. Who else felt? Possibly every slaveholder in the South, with others who may have sympathized with them. But did these together constitute a majority of the Church or the people? It is very much doubted. But suppose they did.

And what then? Must the highest judicature of the Church, to propitiate them, put to death, on the altar of a pseudo expediency, essential moral principle—an expediency that thus gives the go-by to the good pleasure of the Divine will, to secure the good pleasure of these three hundred thousand slaveholders—and that too in an unnatural and unchristian tyranny over two millions of their species? Never! no, never! If the General Conference had sought to array the Church against the State, or said that the Southern ministry and membership, who, in the providential circumstances of their existence, are unavoidably connected with the evil of slavery, are not good ministers and good Christians; or that it is not the business of the Southern States to manage this whole question as their wisdom and goodness shall determine for the best,—then there would have been some just ground of complaint. But not one word, no, not one breathing whisper of all this was uttered! What then is the measure of the offence? Why, the General Conference said, that a bishop, whose official character is the property of the whole Church, is unacceptable to the great body of the Church, because he knowingly, avoidably, and contrary to implied faith in his election to that office, voluntarily connected himself with slavery; and that it was the sense of that body that he relieve himself of that embarrassment before he proceed to the further discharge of the duties of the episcopacy;—a request which he, as a Christian bishop, waiving all the other facts in the case, was, on the great law of gospel, not Southern, expediency, bound to regard, either by resigning his office, or freeing himself from slavery.

It may be objected here, that the Church, in her

action in this case, did, in the personal rights of Bishop Andrew, array herself against the State, and, by consequence, against the rights of the entire Southern ministry and membership.

We reply, First, our Discipline, which on this subject is only the utterance of the voice of reason and revelation, declares slavery to be a "great evil." He and they have subscribed to this doctrine; and they act very inconsistently with their profession when they voluntarily connect themselves with it. And it is both the right and duty of the Church to protect herself in the premises.

Secondly. If the laws of the State have established a practical principle in contravention of essential right, and which Christianity, for the time being, in view of the "weakness of the flesh," tolerates in those unavoidably connected with it, a layman has no Christian right, much less a Christian bishop, voluntarily to connect himself with it, and then seek to justify and defend his conduct on the ground of civil rights.

It may be urged here, that in our mixed condition, this is a point of great delicacy to come under Church jurisdiction. This will be readily admitted. But we are inclined to the opinion, that too much importance has been attached to it. We are perfectly willing that it shall pass for all it is worth, but nothing more. That by way of accommodation to our fallen condition, the dispensations of our Maker have come down in astonishing lengths, is not denied. Everything is done that could be done, without giving up essential moral principle. And if we, in view of this gracious stoop, voluntarily connect ourselves with any palpable wrong, it is to presume on the mercy of God, and to "sin that grace may abound;" and by consequence to fall under all the weight, and be chargeable with all the guilt involved in the Apostle's argument on this subject. But you object to the charge of sinfulness in such a step, claiming that the civil law has established the relation, and that when thus established the gospel tolerates it, and therefore it is your right, as a citizen, to claim and act upon that right. We have already, in a civil point of view, conceded this right. But in reference to your Christian right to do so, the question which here comes up is, when examined in the light of the laws of nature, and pure Christianity, is the civil law which establishes the relation based on essential right? And does the gospel tolerate it in that sense? If such are the facts in the case, such is your right, and you do right in acting upon that right. But we reply, that we think we have already proved beyond all controversy, that the laws establishing the relation are not founded on right, and that the gospel does not tolerate the relation in the sense of right. The question then here is, Is it the Christian right of any man, with his eyes open to all the facts in the case, voluntarily and practically to connect himself with a principle which is in contravention of the laws of eternal rectitude, simply because the gospel, on the ground of civil rights, tolerates it in those who, in the providential circumstances of their existence, are unavoidably connected with it? To grant this is, for aught we can see to the contrary, to surrender the whole government of God. For on this principle it is only necessary for the civil law to establish any grossly immoral principle or practice; and on the ground of civil rights, we may, as Christians, adopt the one, or conform to the other. To us, it appears to be absolutely impossible to get away from this conclusion.

To deny this right, is to charge those who have claimed and acted on it with sin, a violation of this great law of Christianity, which is based on essential moral principle, and all the guilt consequent upon so fearful a departure from the rules of moral rectitude; which, on the supposition that they knew the law, must, in view of the consequences involved, be immense, not to say immeasurable. How has such a course obscured the moral glory of Christianity! How has it strengthened the bands of slavery! The single case of Bishop Andrew is, and would have been much more so, but for the rebuke it met with from the Church, an apology—yea more, a cordial to the conscience of every human monster that trades in the bodies and souls of men—of every slaveholder that fattens on the gains of their sweat, and toil, and blood—and of every unprincipled driver that lends himself to the dirty work of plying the bloody lash. They will reason, Why, the Bishop, one of the earthly spiritual heads of a large and prosperous Church—a Church that claims to have been "raised up to spread Scriptural holiness over these lands," is into it. And surely, as Dr. Elliot says, "it must be a holy thing." And thus they will strengthen their hearts in their position, and feel quite complacent in view of their honourable and holy company. This is neither a far-fetched nor weak conclusion; we appeal to the intelligence of the world for its truth and support.

And if this one instance is fraught with such disastrous consequences, how great is the breach in this branch of public morals, in view of the Hardings and others in the ministry and membership, who have voluntarily connected themselves with this species of iniquity! And how alarmingly fearful is the whole system of American slavery, strengthened by the recent action and present position of the Church South! What would-be or actual slaveholder but now feels himself hedged about as with bulwarks of salvation? that he is shielded, defended, and protected by the whole weight of their influence, and the broad sanction that influence has given to the principle and practice of slavery? Brethren, pause and look around you!

And when examined in the light of Scripture, reason, and truth, as set forth in these pages, of what avail are the so-called *compromise laws*, as interpreted by the South? Mark! when those compromise laws are simply understood as covering the case of those who, in the providential circumstances of their existence, are unavoidably connected with slavery, we believe them to be correct; that in this sense they are in perfect accordance with Scripture and reason. But the South go further, and claim as their right, secured by these compromise laws, that their members, preachers, and bishops, as in the case of Harding and Andrew, may monopolize at will, by marriage, gift, and otherwise, all this species of property. Now, is it a rational conclusion that such was the design of the framers of those laws, to say nothing about our ecclesiastical laws, which declare and brand it as a "great evil?" Is there the least shadow of evidence that such could have been their purpose? And when we look at those compromise laws in the light of her general standing laws on the subject of slavery, which mark it as a "great evil," declare the ineligibility of all slaveholders to any official station in the Church, when the laws of the State in which they live will admit of emancipation, and permit the liberated slave to enjoy freedom; and which further work the forfeiture of the ministerial character of any travelling preacher who by ANY MEANS becomes the owner of a slave or slaves, unless he execute, if practicable, a legal emancipation of such slaves, conformably to the laws of the State in which he may reside; and in the face of all this, for it now to be claimed that these same laws were intended to shield men who, in the providential circumstances of their existence, were free from it, in a voluntary connexion with it, is entirely out of the question. It is absolutely impossible, with any degree of reason or plausibility, to suppose such to have been their design. What! the assembled wisdom of a whole religious body, full of godly wisdom, met in grave and prayerful deliberation for the good of the Church, the promotion of the kingdom of Christ in the world—then and there solemnly (the South themselves aiding and abetting) to conspire, not secretly, but by public law, not only to nullify their own law, but on the altar of an expediency which "does evil that good may come," to commit high treason against the government of God? Impossible! No sound impartial mind can so understand it. The thought is too monstrous, too shocking for rational belief; and the South should have more regard for themselves than to urge it.

But should we, for the sake of argument, admit the claims of the South in this matter, can they, will they, in view of the principles involved, claim to abide these laws, and that the Church is to be governed by them? They cannot do this with impunity, on any other ground than by first proving our position wrong, and establishing the doctrine that a man has a Christian right to do whatever the civil laws may legalize; —that is, require or permit him to do. So far as we can see, there is no alternative. And failing to do this, can it be they are so in love with, wedded to, and blind as to the true character of the system, that they are ready to make any sacrifice of principle to sustain it, and thus, before all earth and heaven, "crucify to themselves the Son of God afresh, and put him to an open shame?" We repeat, are they prepared for such a consummation as this? We hope not. We entertain more charitable views of the Southern Church, ministry, and people. Our solemn conviction is, that they have not understood the true position of slavery in the Divine administration; and, therefore, they have wholly overlooked this great law of Christianity which is involved in the question. Such, we repeat, is our honest conviction of the causes which have misled the South. Our mantle of charity is big enough to cover every case but Bishop Andrew's;—and him too, in this particular aspect of the question. It is the last thing we would dare to do, to throw away any man, in a moral point of view, much less a whole body of Christian ministers and people, while there is any rational ground on which their conduct can be explained. There are other facts so notoriously outstanding in the Bishop's case, that our mantle of charity cannot cover him. Out of his own mouth we judge him! His having stated on the floor of the General Conference that Brother Winans told him he could not vote for him, because he was nominated as a Southern man, free from slavery, and by consequence, that his election was to proceed on that principle, settles the question. As an honourable man, leaving Christianity out of the question, it was his solemn duty then and there, at the time of his election to the episcopate, publicly to have protested against the principle; or, when he afterwards did connect himself with slavery, to have resigned, or at least to have tendered his office to the body that conferred it. There positively was no alternative—no other way under the heavens for him to save his character from just aspersion. And after all himself and his friends can do, it is utterly out of the question to shield him from guilt, and the just condemnation of enlightened, intelligent, and public opinion.

We may be regarded as pressing this case too hard. Our reply is, that the offence is public and outstanding, and is of such a nature, because of the peculiar position of the perpetrator, that to pass over it in smooth and honeyed phrase would be treason to truth and the Church of God. And we feel deeply conscious before God, that the interests at stake fully protect us from the charge of "evil speaking," in the undisguised utterance of our sober convictions in this matter. And we hope we shall ever have independence enough, when the truth requires it, to "know no man after the flesh," whether bishop, priest, or deacon.

All things considered, abating, as a matter of taste, one figure used, no speech delivered before the General Conference, on this unhappy question, pleased us better than John Spencer's, of the Pittsburg Conference, (or brother Cass's, judging from his beginning,) simply because it sought to meet the case on its merits. And that man who writes the history of the Church, including the doings of that General Conference, and does not give it a corresponding notice, will fail of his duty.

And when we bring that ever to be lamented plan of division to the standard of moral and Christian truth,—the great law of Christianity for which we here contend,—and measure its dimensions, and ascertain its character by this test, in what light does it appear? Why, a sundering the bonds of Christian union and fellowship, on the altar of a pseudo expediency. Not one word was said by the North, in derogation of the Christian or ministerial character of those unavoidably connected with the slavery relation. Their position was against the voluntary connexion, on his part, of one of their bishops with slavery. And the position of the South was, that such was his right, such was to be expected from his location as a southern man, and that the compromise laws fully covered his case. We think, however, that we have demonstrably proved to the contrary, so clearly so, that the South will, for their own sakes, as Christians and Christian ministers, abandon it. But suppose they do not, and still urge those compromise laws; our reply is, that the great law of Christianity now under consideration does not cover it, but brands it with essential iniquity; and as the result, what are the respective positions of the parties at issue? Why, the North stands high up on the elevation of moral principle, truth, and goodness, so as to be read and known by an intelligent universe, as being in the right. And the South, so far as principle is concerned, away down deep in hell, apparently enveloped in a darkness so profound, as to render their opacity impenetrable by the rays of moral glory which so flame out from this principle as to give light to all the world beside. True, the mists, and fogs, and smoke that were raised, connected with the exciting character of the question, seem to have disqualified the great portion of the North for that clear and calm deliberation that is necessary to those nice discriminations, which ascertain and follow truth in those new channels of duty which time and circumstances evolve. And hence they were found on the contingency, that it, in the future, should be ascertained to be necessary for the good of the Church, giving a reluctant assent to this measure. The motive was a laudable one, and gives character to the action, and is therefore their apology, although the act, in itself, was essentially wrong. However, in their sober second thoughts, they have done the best that fallible mortals can do; discovering their error, they, by seizing upon the first opportunity to repeal the odious measure, have confessed and forsaken that error.

We might, in the next place, give a moment's attention to a question before alluded to. We mean the overture tendered by the South for fraternal relations, under the circumstances which mark the history of the respective positions of the parties to this question: Did the North do right in rejecting that overture? To answer this question we must ask another. Have the South, as we contend, in the position they have taken, surrendered the government of God, by setting up a spurious expediency unknown to Christianity, and thus made void the law of God through their traditions? If such be the fact, and we challenge them to disprove it, would not the action of the North, in receiving and reciprocating the fraternal overture, be to endorse their position, and, by so doing, to surrender this principle of the Divine government? Such, for aught we can see to the contrary, is the conclusion that logically flows from the premises; and in view of which fact, it was their imperative duty to reject the overture tendered, under the pains and penalties of high treason to the Divine government.

And examined in the light of this principle, is the North justified in establishing conferences within the jurisdiction of the slaveholding States? Our reply to this interrogatory is, that in the surrender of this high moral principle to a time-serving expediency, which claims to "do evil that good may come," they have, so far as this principle is concerned, given the go-by to the gospel Paul preached. And does not he say, "If an angel from heaven should preach any other gospel, let him be accursed?" The application is easy. Tested by this principle, the question is easily answered, and must be answered in the affirmative.

And yet once more, with regard to their antagonistic position. We now allude to the legal controversy pending,—a grave matter, and one which, on Christian principles, and among a Christian people, never can be justified, only by the most clear and outstanding reasons of right and fitness. If the question is involved in doubt, it might be in accordance with Christian principle to submit it amicably, for legal arbitrament; but in no case, or under no circumstances, is it compatible with the principles and spirit of Christianity, to undertake the adjustment of questions thus involved in doubt, in the spirit of litigation. In a case of clear outstanding right, where one party, in open violation of that right, persisted in holding on to any advantage that circumstances may have given them, the party complaining might, in this aspect of the question, be justified in an appeal to Cæsar. Let us here inquire if the suit now pending, as instituted by the South, is of this character,—if it possesses this unequivocal, authenticating claim, either in a legal or moral point of view.

First, legal. As growing out of obvious, unequivocal ecclesiastical law. Now we think this cannot be maintained, because, first, a majority of the General Conference, who are, when convened, the constitutional interpreters of their own acts, have, when thus assembled, declared, by the solemn vote of a large majority, that the so-called compromise laws were not intended to protect a bishop in voluntarily connecting himself with slavery. And, second, because of its unreasonableness. It being, in effect, a nullification of the other standing laws of the Church on the subject of slavery, which brand and treat it as a great wrong.

Second, moral. As having the support and sanction of essential moral principle. This also we think cannot be maintained, for the following reasons:

1. It has as its only basis, a conventional article or plan of division, extorted in the hour of confusion and hurried excitement, as a contingency to meet possible, future, apprehended difficulties.

2. This contingency was forthwith acted upon, by the issue of a call for a convention of the Church, composed of the slaveholding States, in contravention of the faith of the party assenting to it merely as a contingency, the necessity of which, time and circumstances must determine.

3. The contingency itself, should it, in the developments of time and circumstances, be found necessary, in accordance with the faith of the assenting party, is based on an illegitimate expediency, subversive of essential moral principle; which in itself, apart from the aforementioned reasons but particularly in connexion

with them, brands it as not having the support or sanction of gospel morality. And if, as we think we have here proved, it shall be found that the suit now in progress has neither the sanction of law or morals, can the South proceed one step further in a course so essentially wrong, and still lay claim to the character of Christians? We think not.

Should they continue in their present position, everything that can be done without giving up essential moral principle should be done, to give them their portion of the goods. And now, brethren, to close this long address, as before intimated, "I wot that in ignorance ye have done these things;" that is, without a correct understanding of the question of slavery, and the principles involved in the course you have taken. Weigh well the doctrines of these pages, and the arguments by which they are sustained. Examine them in the light of Scripture and reason. If you can, answer and refute them. If you cannot, retrace your steps.

CONCLUSION.

"Let us hear the conclusion of the matter." Well, as has been already stated, there are two great classes of truth, or law, which govern this relation, and which are to be kept steadily in view if, in our investigation of this subject, we would be conducted to safe and satisfactory conclusions; a want of attention to which has, as we think, greatly contributed to the confusion and darkness in which this question seems yet to be involved. And,

First. They are the great essential laws of right and eternal rectitude, in the sense of immutable truth, as pertaining to the first constitution of things.

Second. The great laws of Christianity, or the principles of a remedial government.

The first law, or constitution of things, determines slavery to be essentially wrong.

The second law keeps up essentially the same idea, but directs how to manage that wrong when and where it is found in existence.

This brief analysis seems to us to be Scriptural and rational, and as commending itself to the sober judgment of all men as such.

Now, as it appears to us, the extremes of this question are as follows:—

The ultraism of abolition plants itself on unbending moral law, and measures the whole question by this rule. This is correct, so far as the principle is concerned; and will equally apply to all other wrong principles which have obtained in the history of our fallen world. But is this the rule on which the Divine government, as now constituted, proceeds? Is there no regard paid to the providential circumstances of our existence—our ignorance, our unavoidable connexion with evil, &c.? Why, on all other subjects, the principles of a remedial government apply; but on this subject there is no grace in any of its phases, for, says the Rev. Edward Smith, "Slavery is essentially man-stealing under all circumstances," and as such a soul-damning sin; and the person or persons connected therewith—though, so far as the circumstances which originated the evil, and by which it was first made, and continues to be, an element of the social and civil state, are as innocent as the angels in heaven—cannot have a place in the Church of God; and therefore the apostles never admitted them to its communion and fellowship.

Pro-slaveryism plants itself on unlimited and irresponsible grace; and claims, in contravention of the law of nature and eternal rectitude, a Divine right to practise on the principle; and thus wholly overlooks the great design of the gospel, as a gracious expedient to restore us back as fully, in spirit and practice, to primitive rectitude as is consistent with our fallen condition,—the consummation of which must, in its onward march, sweep away slavery, and every other refuge of lies, which, under the dominion and prevalence of sin, has obtained in the world. And also forgets that the Gospel tolerates it temporarily, only in view of this reaction of grace, and holds us responsible, as Christians, for the fulfilment of the law of nature and eternal rectitude as fully, both in spirit and practice, as can be done in the providential circumstances of our gracious existence: "That the righteousness of the law might be fulfilled in us; who walk not after the flesh, but after the Spirit."

Now, as it appears to us, the truth lies between these extremes. The law judges the character of slavery; the gospel, the circumstances of our connexion with it. The law proclaims the slave's right to freedom; the gospel shows us how, and sets us to work, not by acts of violence, but on principles of moral goodness, to bring about that freedom.

This, as before remarked, seems to us to be the only rational view we can take of this question; and hence the ecclesiastical polity of Methodism, which, as before stated, is in recognition of both these laws, demonstrates her position to be Scriptural and rational; as well as the folly, not to say the wickedness, of her detractors, both in the North and South.

And now we have done. Not that we have said all that might be said; nor yet that we would claim exemption from all imperfections, either in style or sentiment. This would be too much to expect in a work written mainly in the interval of hours snatched from the labours of the field by day, or rest by night. We simply mean that we have said what we have deemed necessary to place this question in a Scriptural and rational light before the Church and world; and are unfeignedly conscious of not having designedly attempted to pervert or suppress our sober convictions of truth.

That it shall escape censure, is not to be expected; nor yet that the author's motives will not be impugned. We desire that it may be tried by the closest scrutiny, as to doctrine; and if, when weighed in the balances of the sanctuary and reason, it shall be found wanting, that it may receive its just demerits. We commend it to the reader, and commit it to its fate, humbly praying that it may subserve the cause of truth and righteousness; and shall patiently await the verdict of calm, deliberate, intelligent public opinion.

THE END.

www.ingramcontent.com/pod-product-compliance
Lightning Source LLC
LaVergne TN
LVHW010237110826
845151LV00004B/1321
9781425524180